Patchwork Rounds of Friendship

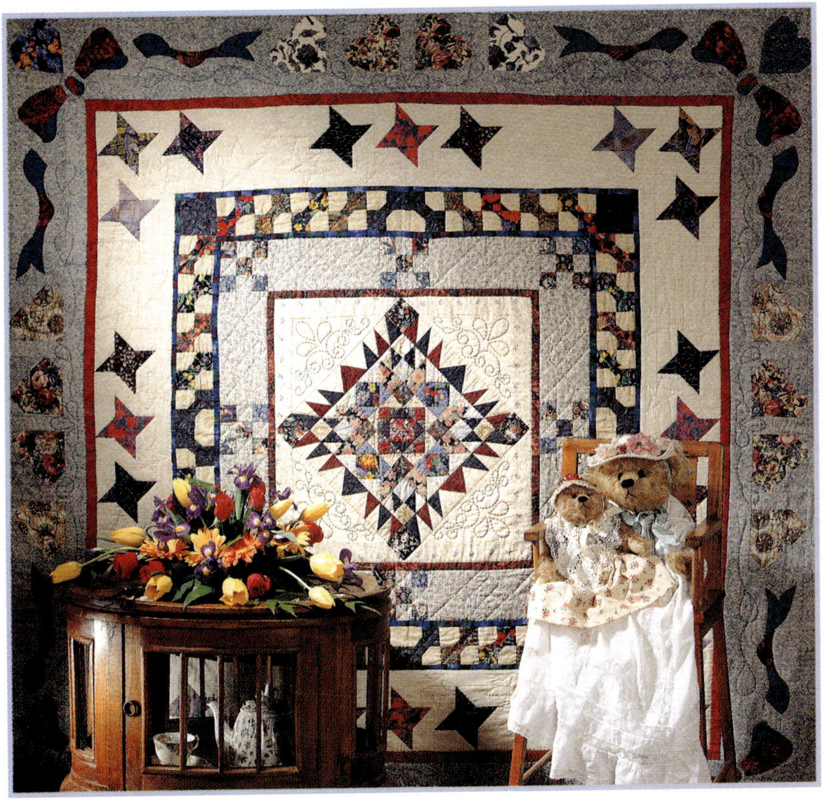

Sharing the Joys of Quilt Making with

Debbie Herd
Frances Morris
Margaret Bryden
Rebecca Pring
Elizabeth Matsen
Liz Grabham
Narelle Elloy
Yan Pring

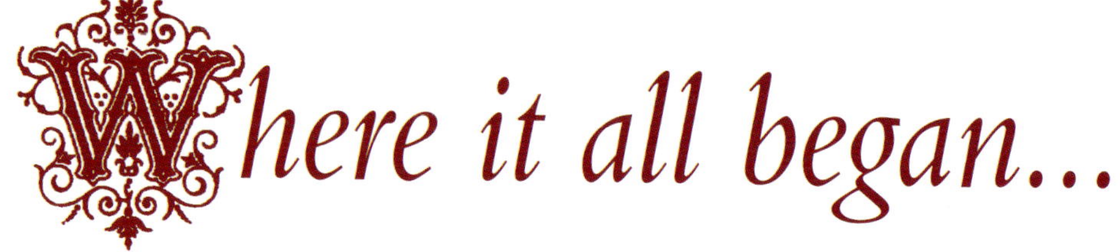

True friendship is not a 'fad'
Is not 'in season'
It lasts forever
Without a reason.

Evelyn Axtell Barrows

The group, who like to be thought of as 'evening bags', are mostly referred to as just 'the hags'. We are fabric lovers often found with no food in the cupboards and threads on our clothes. We make time to meet regularly – inspiring, encouraging and supporting one another as true friends. Over the years we have not only shared our fabric, but also our laughter and tears.

A new excitement possessed the group in late 1994 after reading *Round Robin Quilts* by Pat Maixner Margaret and Donna Ingram Slusser, published by That Patchwork Place. We then felt ready to try a pass-around project. We knew we possessed enthusiasm! We hoped for the flexibility to work together harmoniously and we were keen to prove our commitment.

Using the helpful guidelines in the book, we kept our rules simple and gave ourselves a year to complete the task. As we worked on one another's quilts we set ourselves higher standards, perfecting piecing techniques, stretching our design skills and pushing creativity to new limits. We learned to be patient, tolerant and to meet deadlines. The joys at the end cannot be expressed in words – the wonderful quilts that are now our own, speak for themselves.

Our very special thanks to Anne's Glory Box, our constant source of supplies and inspiration and the provider of the fabulous venue for our Hand-over Day.

Debbie, Elizabeth, Frances, Lizzie, Margaret, Narelle, Rebecca and Yan.

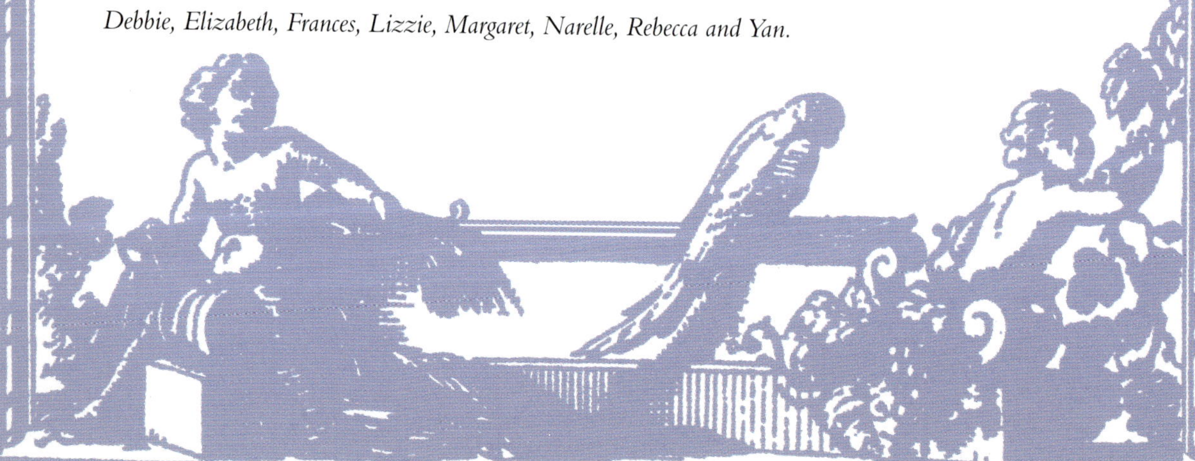

Contents

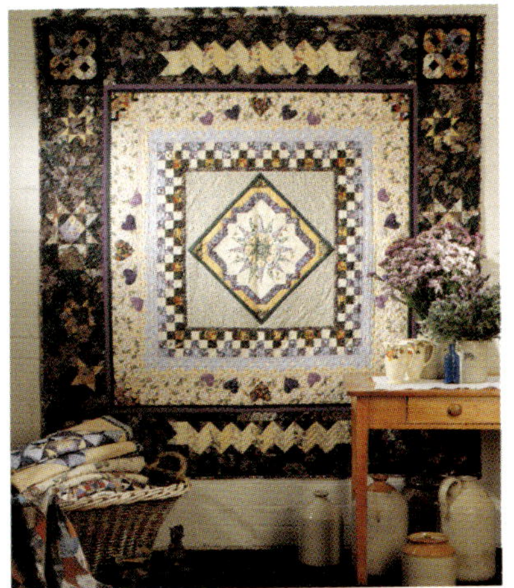

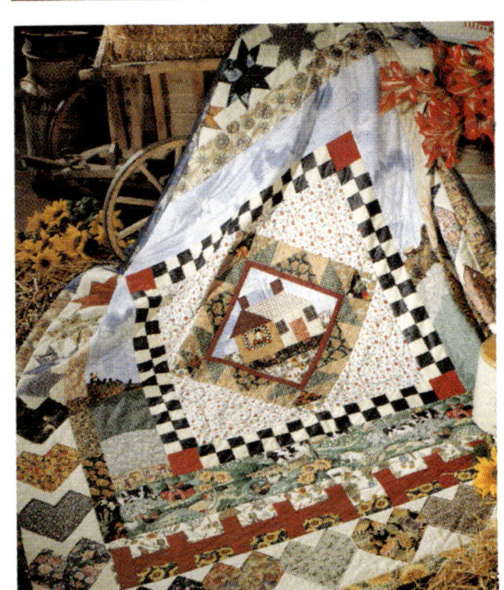

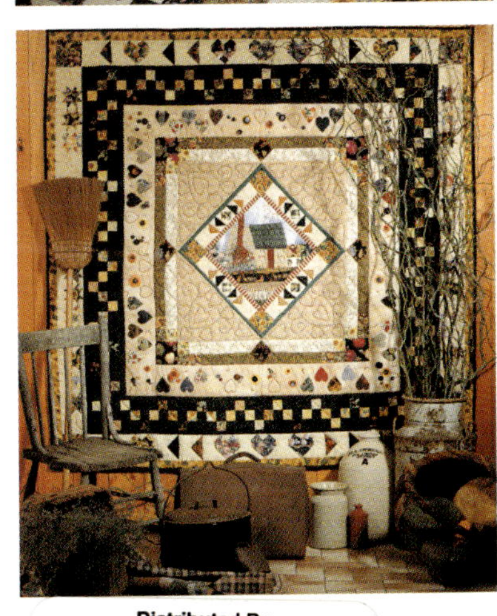

Distributed By
Quilters' Resource Inc.
Chicago, IL 60614
1-800-676-6543

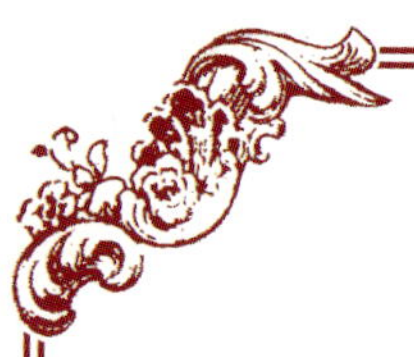
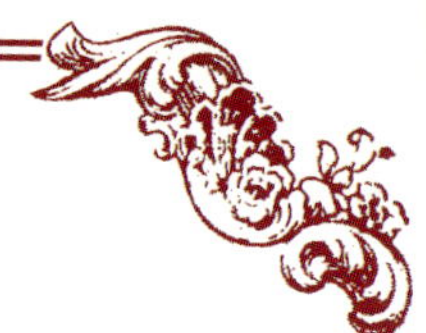

Getting Started

The wonderful journey began with a hand-out sheet setting out the basic rules and a recipe containing simple guidelines for the month-by-month rounds.

THE RULES

- Do not show the owner her quilt at any time
- You may consult with other members
- Be committed and ready to pass-on each month and be willing to share (ideas and fabric)
- DON'T winge, whine or wince
- Expect to own a beautiful quilt

THE RECIPE

Month 1 Construct your own block (12in x 12in finished)
Month 2 Border with triangles (approx 3in width)
Month 3 Turn on point, add four corner triangles to make a square
Month 4 A design containing squares and/or rectangles
Month 5 Something pretty (approximately 5in wide)
Month 6 A design based on a nine-patch block
Month 7 Add two sides with stars
Month 8 Add two sides with hearts
Month 9 Receive your quilt
Month 10 Add more if you wish and complete the quilt

We passed-on in rotation from an alphabetical name list. Group participants were consistently keen to sight the progress at each "pass-on" session – the quilt owner being more than cooperative to leave the room while this took place.

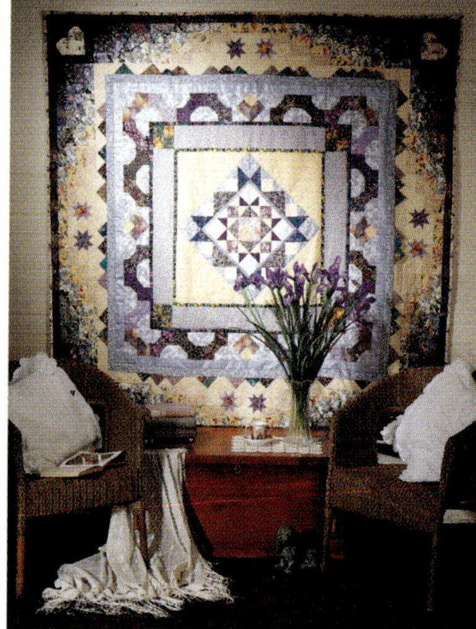

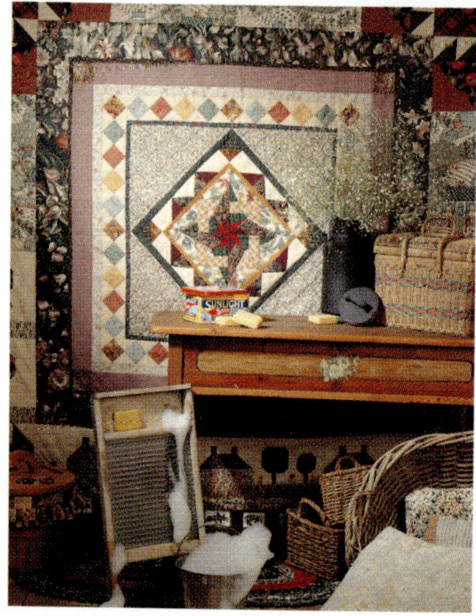

The recipe proved flexible enough in content and time frame to cater for individual abilities, and the unexpected and unpredictable events that life so often presents. When a round was completed ahead of schedule an early "pass-on" gave valuable extra time. When time was needed to be extended beyond the schedule, agreement was reached between the participants concerned.

Each month we experienced a deepening of our commitment, an expansion of our tolerance and a boost to our confidence as we shared pattern ideas, fabric, books, magazines, sketches, notes and phone calls.

THE GOLDEN RULE

"Work on another's quilt as you would want them to work on yours." This rule lifted our standards to greater heights and our personal bests became better.

We acknowledge the marvellous helpful information in *Round Robin Quilts* by Pat Maixner Margaret and Donna Ingram Slusser.

It is a manual for a successful project and makes highly recommended reading.

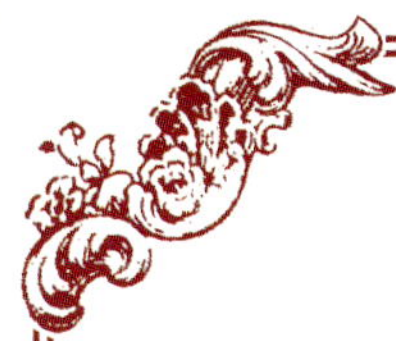

MAKING THE QUILTS

- It is difficult to provide quantities for the quilt projects as many different fabrics were used to give charm and sparkle. It is suggested you work with your favourite colour schemes in a 'scrap bag' selection – blending tones and adding prints from your own collection or indulging in the pleasure of purchasing extras as needed. In a group activity sharing-the-stash is beneficial and provides an extensive range of fabric at no extra cost.
- Imperial measurements are used for templates and cutting instructions. Remember to add ¼in (6mm) seam allowance on all templates.
- For accuracy and speed use rotary cutters, ruler and mat when cutting fabric for your projects.
- 'Finished size' means after the seams have been stitched together.
- 'Cut a strip' means across from selvedge to selvedge of 45in (115cm) wide fabric.
- 'Float' means an extra fabric strip added to an edge section of the quilt. The ½in finished strips are cut 1¼in wide to make handling the narrow strip easier.
- Rounds six and seven are combined in some quilt projects.
- Refer often to the photographs for piecing and placement as you proceed.

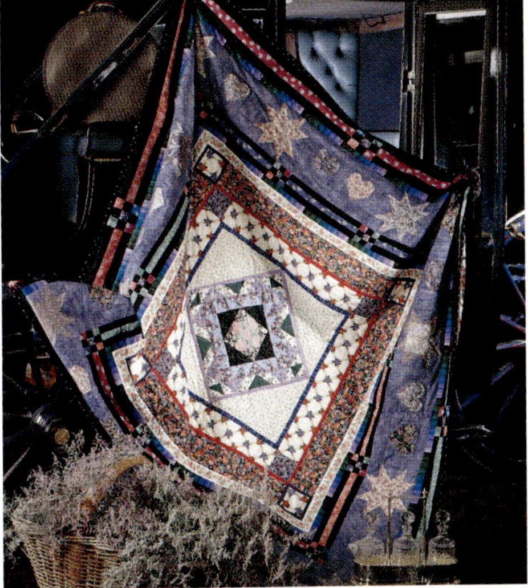

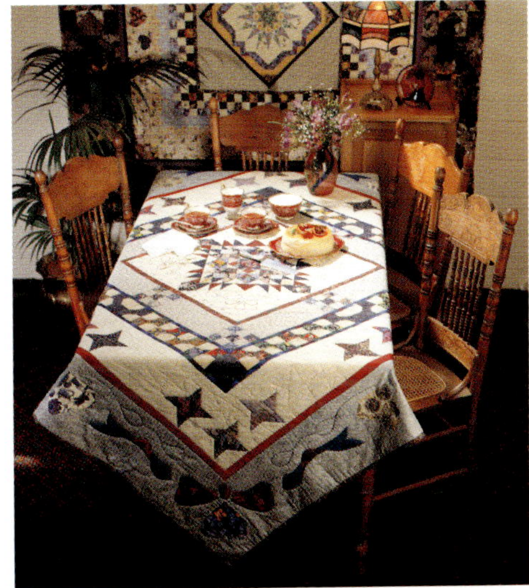

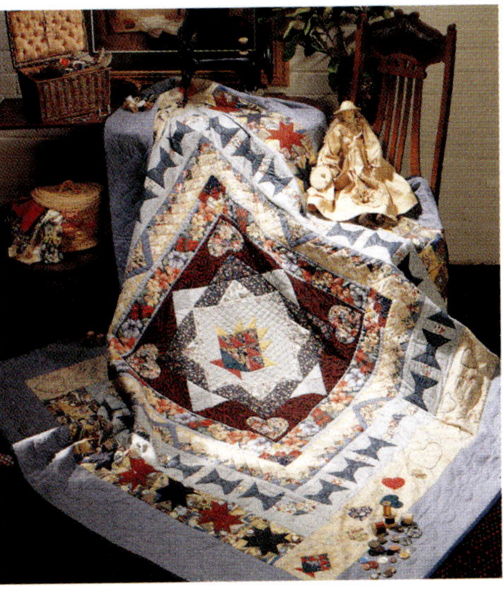

- Templates are made from the patterns provided on the pattern sheet. These templates are finished sizes – always add seam allowance when cutting fabric pieces.
- Select fabrics for the block design including light, medium and dark fabrics, to give the quilt texture and interest. Add plenty of contrasting colours to inspire the coordination of the following rounds. Perhaps your favourite colour(s), in many tones, will feature throughout the project.
- Some of the more complex centre blocks are ideally suited to English piecing. See Basic Instructions.
- After completing each round, press carefully. Do not stretch your fabric edges as the sides will 'bow' making it difficult to attach the next round.
- As you add each new round, float strips may be used to make any necessary adjustments when sides are too short. Gently ease in any extra fullness, taking care there are no tucks or puckers visible, if a side is too long.
- Instructions are for quilt tops only – for further information see the Basic Instructions section to complete your quilt.
- On return of the quilts to the owners, embellishments such as embroidery, appliqué and buttons have been added. The quilts have been backed, bound and quilted by the owners as desired.

Take a deep breath and remember – laughter is the closest thing to flying. Good luck and enjoy your trip!

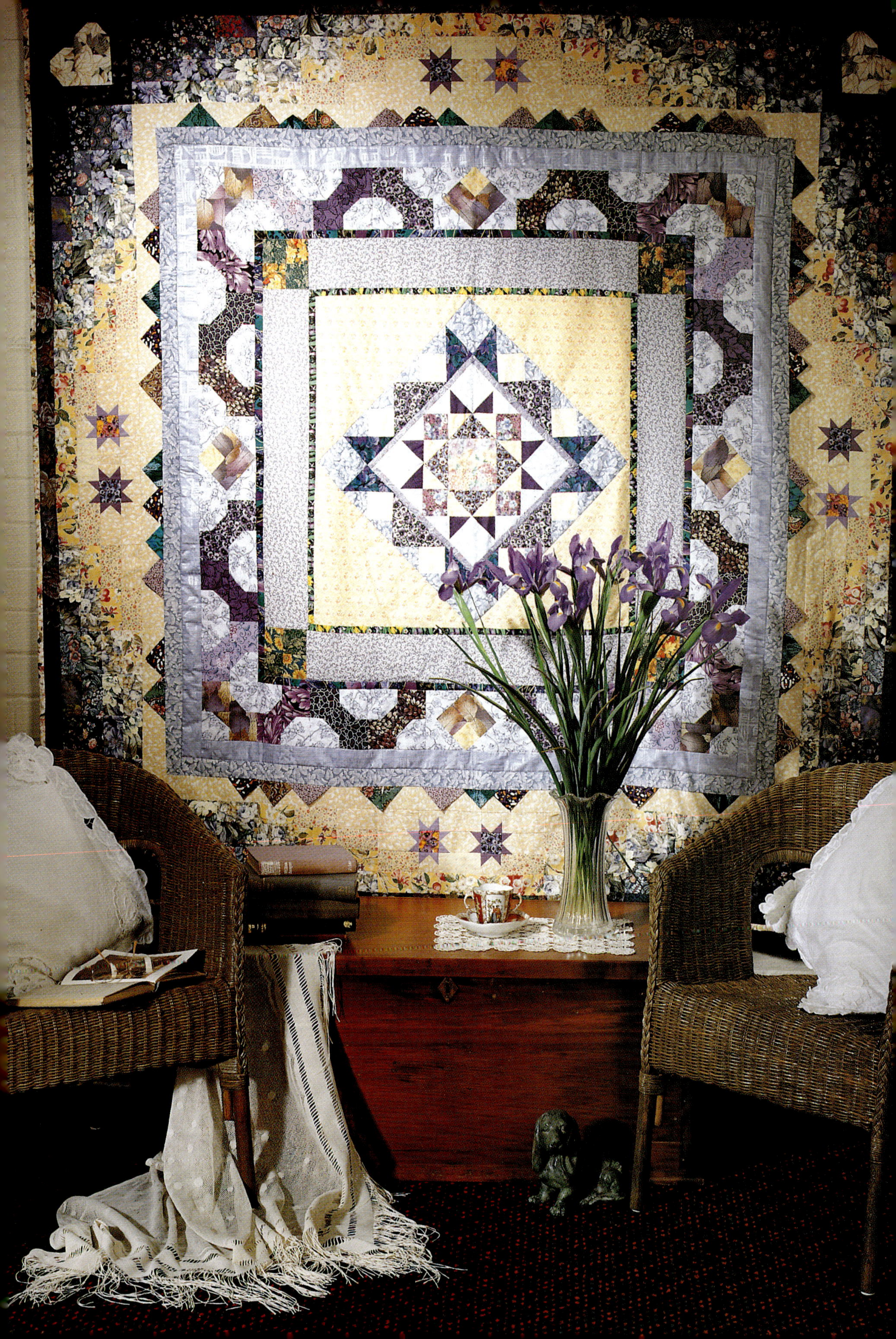

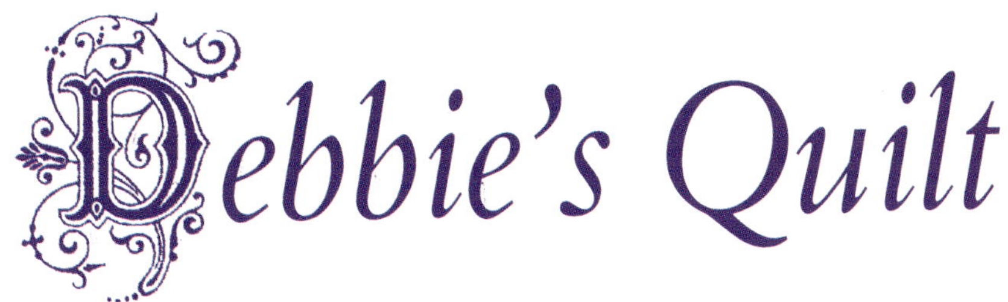

Debbie's Quilt

The block at the beginning repeats rich purples, butter yellows and ice blues in tessellated patterns. We begin to think about mosaic tiles in cool temples flooded suddenly with the gentle golden light of morning.

Read the Getting Started and Basic Instructions sections before you begin your quilt.

THE BLOCK

Cut and piece carefully using block templates and the BLOCK DIAGRAM as a guide. Your block should measure 12in x 12in finished when complete.

ROUND ONE

This round uses four templates from the block. Coordinate your fabric selection to include dark, medium and light colours. See photographs for placement of shapes.

ROUND TWO

Follow the instructions given for Round Two in Margaret's quilt including the float strips.

ROUND THREE

Make four four-patch corner blocks with squares cut $2\frac{1}{2}$in x $2\frac{1}{2}$in (cut four squares for each block).The connecting strips between are cut $4\frac{1}{2}$in x 27in. Add a float strip on four sides cut $1\frac{1}{4}$in wide ($\frac{1}{2}$in finished).

ROUND FOUR

Bow-tie blocks are set around the four corners of the quilt with a four-patch on point in the centre of each side. Rich colours are used for bow-ties and the

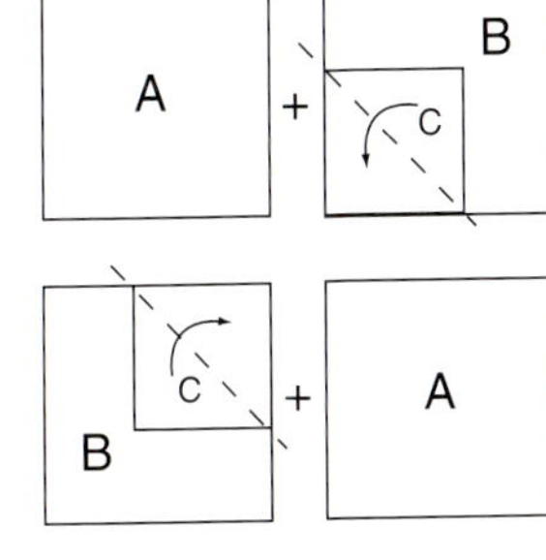

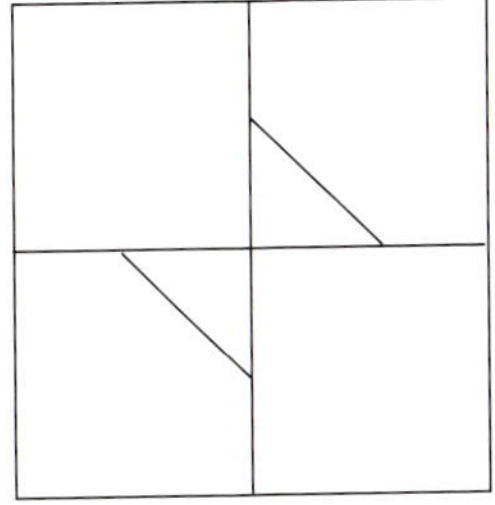

Diagram 1

background fabric is constant (see diagram 1).

Bow-tie Block (make 24)

Cutting sizes:

A. Cut two squares $2\frac{3}{4}$in x $2\frac{3}{4}$in (bow-tie fabric)

B. Cut two squares $2\frac{3}{4}$in x $2\frac{3}{4}$in (background fabric)

C. Cut two squares $1\frac{3}{4}$in x $1\frac{3}{4}$in (bow-tie fabric).

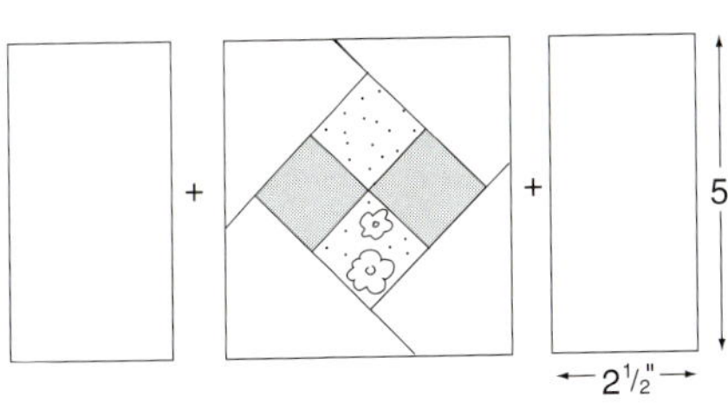

Diagram 2

Connecting Block with four-patch square on point (make 4), see diagram 2.

Cutting sizes:

Four-patch. Cut four 2in x 2in squares (accent fabric)

Cut two squares $3\frac{1}{4}$in x $3\frac{1}{4}$in (background fabric)

Cut each in half diagonally for outer triangles around the four-patch. Rectangles are cut $2\frac{1}{2}$in x 5in (background fabric).

ROUND FIVE

This border is three float strips with prairie-points. The first two float strips are in blue tones. These are cut 2in wide ($1\frac{1}{2}$in finished). The third float strip (yellow) is cut $2\frac{1}{2}$in wide (2in finished). Prairie points are inserted in random groups as you sew on this third float strip. These are made by folding squares of jewel coloured fabrics (see diagram 3).

Prairie-point squares

Cut 3in x 3in

Cut 4in x 4in

Cut 5in x 5in.

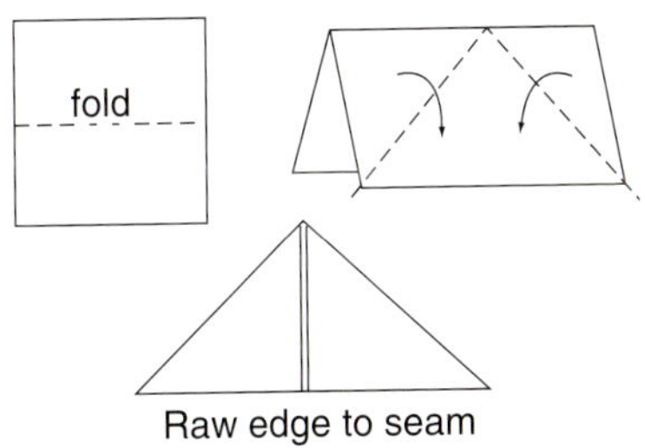

Diagram 3

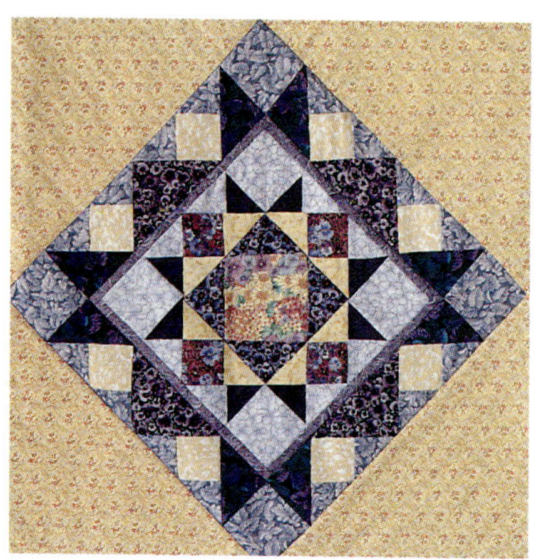

ROUND SIX AND SEVEN

This border is a soft colour-wash of fabrics – light yellows through to dark blues. Select a pleasing blend of prints and cut rectangles $3^3/_4$in x $2^1/_4$in. Follow the layout shown in the photographs. For the heart corners use the pattern in Yan's quilt (diagram 4). Choose light heart fabric and dark background fabric. Float dark background fabric around heart block to make 7in x 7in finished size. For the stars use pattern in Margaret's quilt (diagram 3) with the following new cutting sizes:

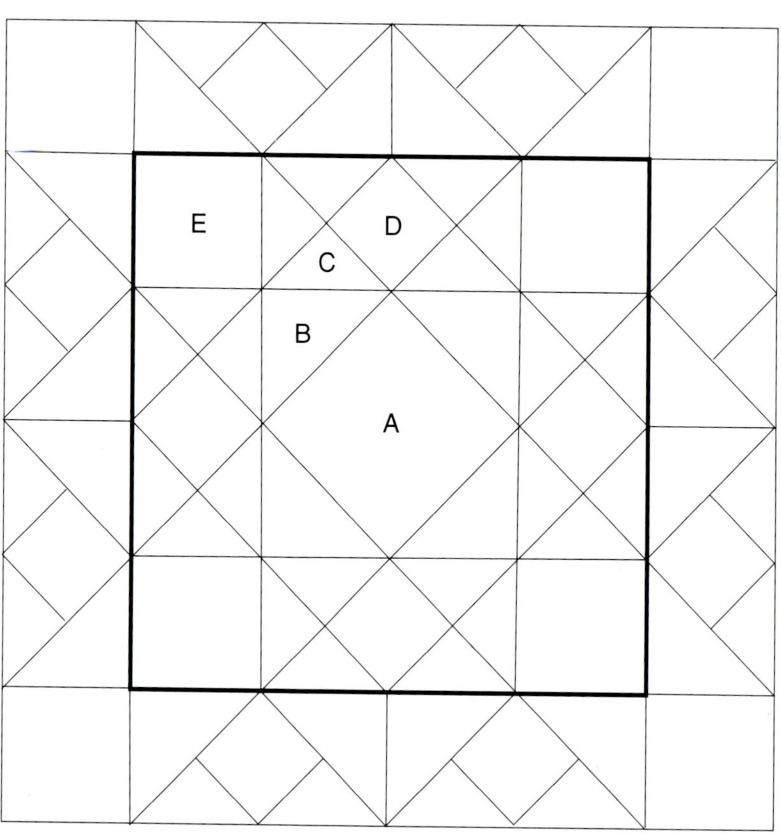

Block Diagram and Round One

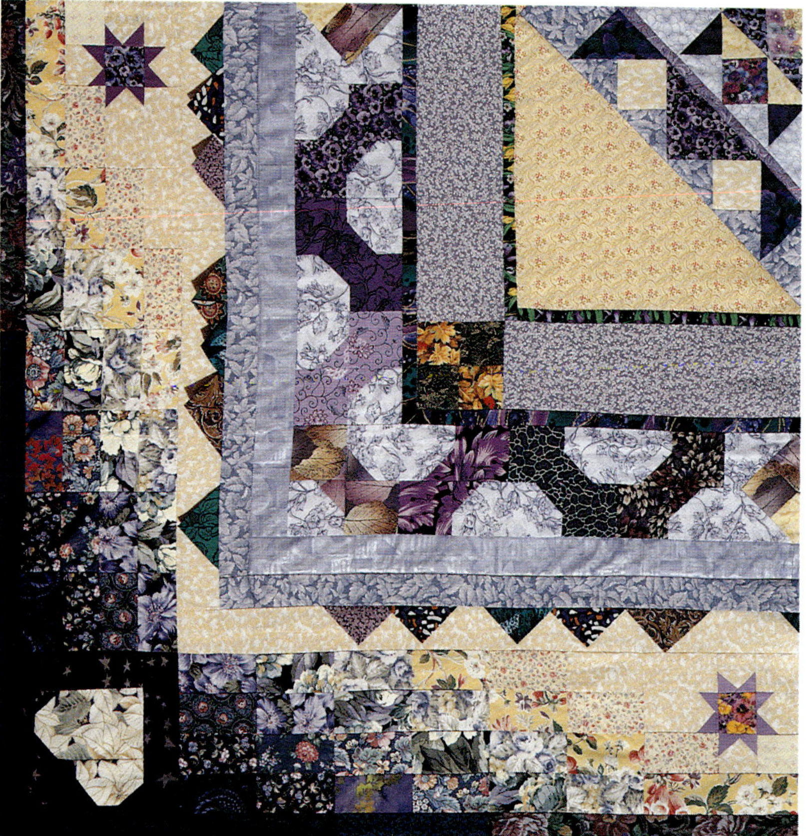

A. Cut one $2^1/_4$in x $2^1/_4$in (star fabric)
B. Cut four $2^1/_4$in x $2^1/_4$in (background fabric)
C. Cut four $2^1/_4$in x $2^1/_4$in (background fabric)
D. Cut eight $1^1/_2$in x $1^1/_2$in (star fabric).

Join star blocks side by side to fit the centre of the colour-wash area (see photographs). Now join all border sections to your quilt. Add one more float strip (cut 2in wide) using various dark prints to complete your quilt.

FINISHED SIZE

72in x 72in (183cm x 183cm)

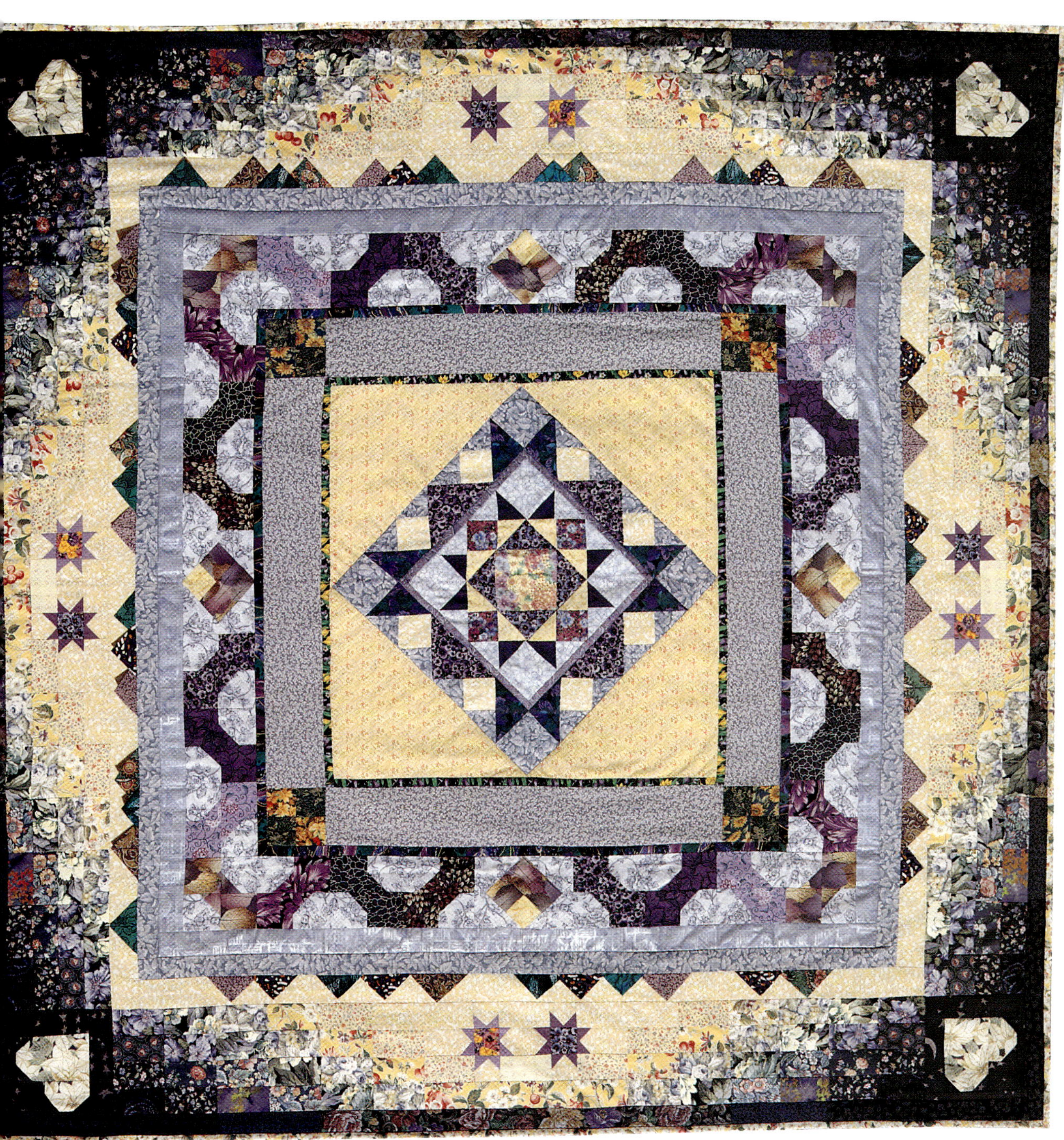

Debbie Herd

Debbie is a tutor in traditional and creative smocking with a special interest in fine embroidery. She has been making quilts for a number of years and also enjoys collecting and making bears. Debbie specialises in original designs in smocking for children's garments.

Elizabeth's Quilt

The block at the beginning is a beautifully executed compass design showing off a starburst of violets, yellows and leafy greens. Honey bees hover in the surroundings, setting the scene for lively ideas of winter gardens.

Read the Getting Started and Basic Instructions sections before you begin your quilt.

THE BLOCK

Cut and piece carefully using the block templates and the BLOCK DIAGRAM as a guide. Your block should measure 12in x 12in finished when complete.

ROUND ONE

Use templates to cut and piece fabrics following the block diagram. Cut float $1\frac{1}{4}$in wide ($\frac{1}{2}$in finished) and sew onto the edges of this round. Remember to add seam allowances to templates.

ROUND TWO

Cut four large triangles as in Round Two Margaret's Quilt.

ROUND THREE

A colour-wash of pretty floral squares repeat in a simple triple. The clever use of cream squares creates a zigzag effect. Cut squares 2in x 2in ($1\frac{1}{2}$in x $1\frac{1}{2}$in finished) and follow the set-up shown in photographs. A float strip is cut to adjust the size between Round Two and Round Three. Elizabeth's Quilt needed a float cut $1\frac{1}{2}$in wide (1in finished). Calculate the width of your strip and sew to the outer edge of the triangles before you join on the assembled squares. Join two short edges first, then two long.

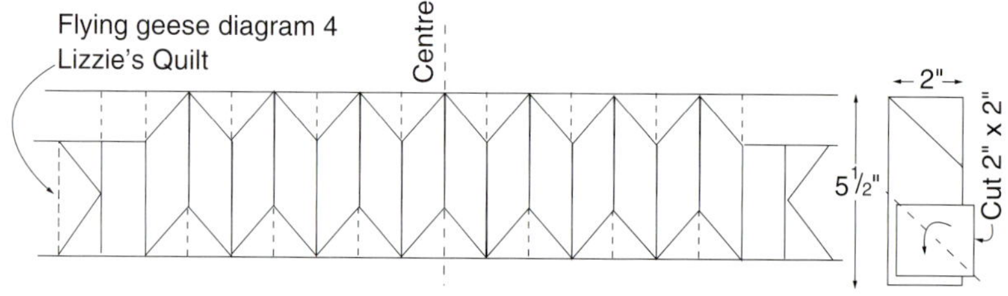

Diagram 1

ROUND FOUR

This simple round makes good use of some very pretty floral fabric. A border print is suitable (as used in the first section of this round). These two wide float strips provide a gentle background for the little hearts. Cut first float strip 4in wide ($3\frac{1}{2}$in finished) and second float strip 5in wide ($4\frac{1}{2}$in finished). Use templates on pattern sheet to make your hearts (remember to add seam allowance). Set them in a shallow curve and appliqué using your favourite technique. The overall effect is an echo of the garland in the centre block.

Optional: Nine-patch colour-wash corners may be used for the corners of the second float. Cut squares 2in x 2in.

Add two dark strips to frame Round Four, first strip cut $1\frac{1}{4}$in ($\frac{1}{2}$in finished) and second strip cut $1\frac{1}{2}$in (1in finished).

ROUND FIVE

This is the final round on Elizabeth's quilt. The background is a rich, muted floral where bright stars flash. The corner blocks again echo the circle in the centre block with four colour-wash rings. Look again and you see elongated chain links – a very clever design.

Simple piecing creates a snappy folded banner in the upper and lower borders. Construct two banners as in diagram 1.

For small stars (upper and lower border) use sizes for stars in Round 6 and 7 Debbie's Quilt.

For medium-sized stars (in side borders) use instructions and sizes in diagram 3 Margaret's Quilt. Leave off alternate points for one pair of stars.

Make large stars using diagram 2 for centres and diagram 3 for construction.

Large star centre (make two)

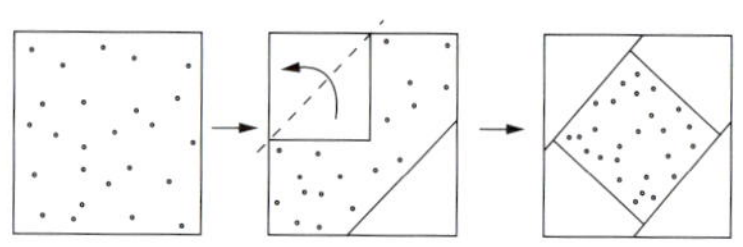

Diagram 2

Cut centre square $5\frac{1}{2}$in x $5\frac{1}{2}$in (star fabric)

Cut four squares $3\frac{1}{2}$in x $3\frac{1}{2}$in

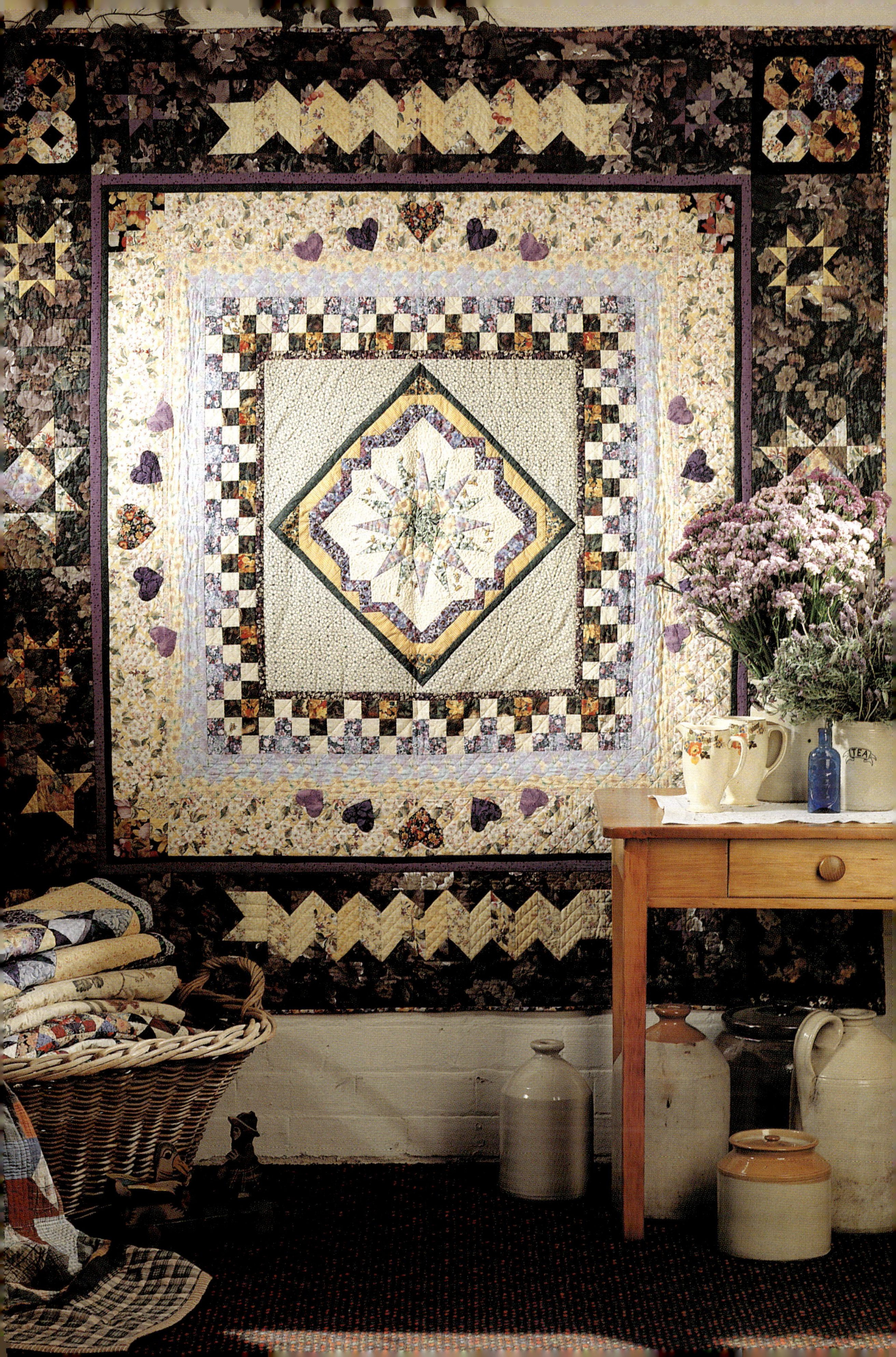
TEA

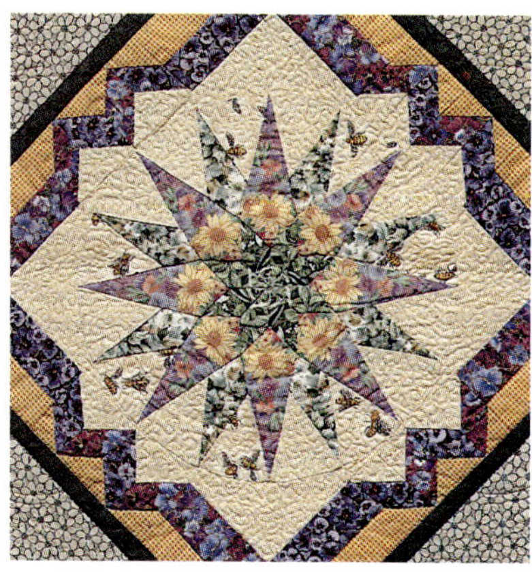

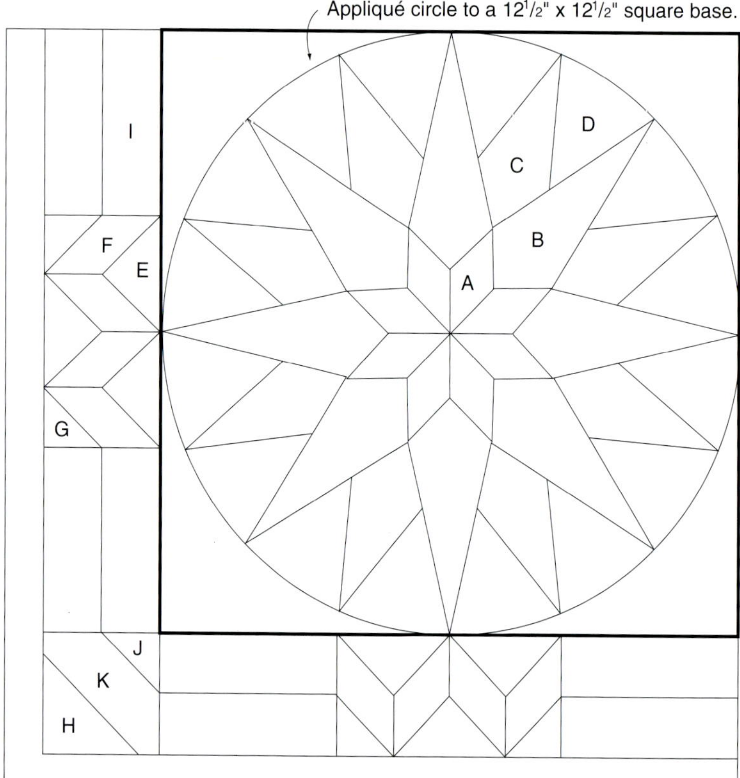

Block Diagram and part of Round One

and place right sides together onto star square, sew diagonally and fold out to form corner triangles.

Use the prepared centres to complete the large stars following diagram 3.

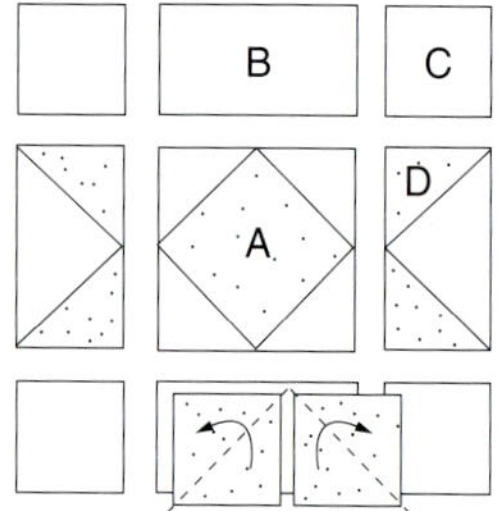

Diagram 3

Large star (make two)

A. Centre square (from diagram 2)

B. Cut four 5½in x 3½in (background fabric)

C. Cut four 3½in x 3½in (background fabric)

D. Cut eight 3½in x 3½in (star fabric).

Float banners and stars in background fabric by calculating, cutting and piecing as you assemble the side of the round. Join with corner blocks made as in diagram 4.

On Elizabeth's Quilt the width of the final border is 11in finished.

2½"

2½"

Cut 1¼" x 1¼"

Diagram 4

FINISHED SIZE

74in x 74in (188cm x 188cm)

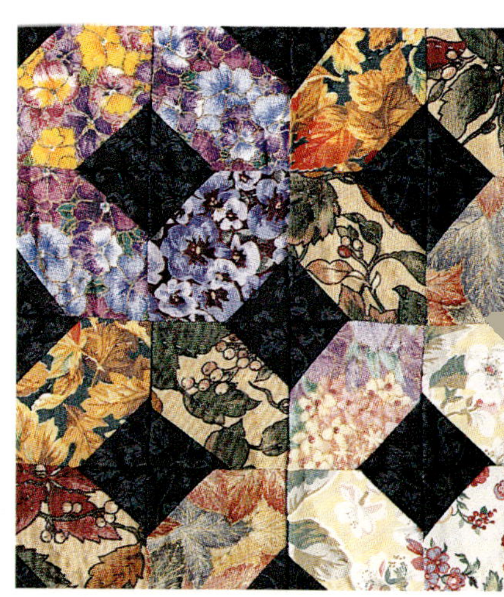

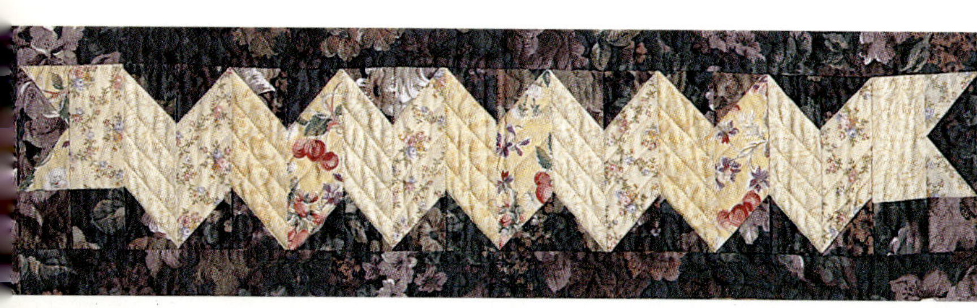

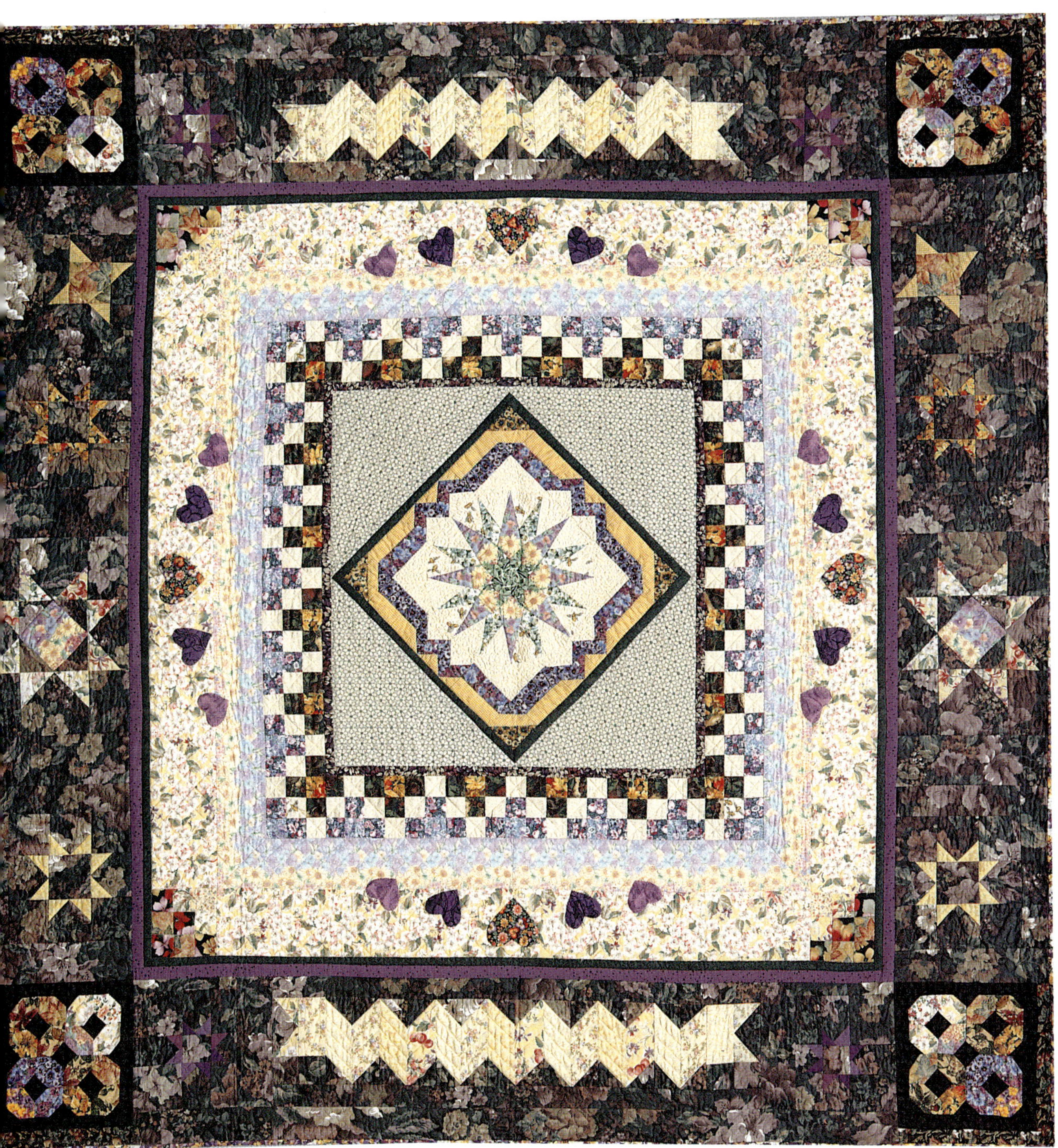

Elizabeth Matsen

Elizabeth began her quilt making when quilt books were rare and classes unavailable. Since then her design and quilting skills, (especially machine quilting) have developed to a high standard. She enjoys making bears and is an enthusiastic member of Hello Dollies Newcastle – exchanging dolls with other doll makers in Australia and USA.

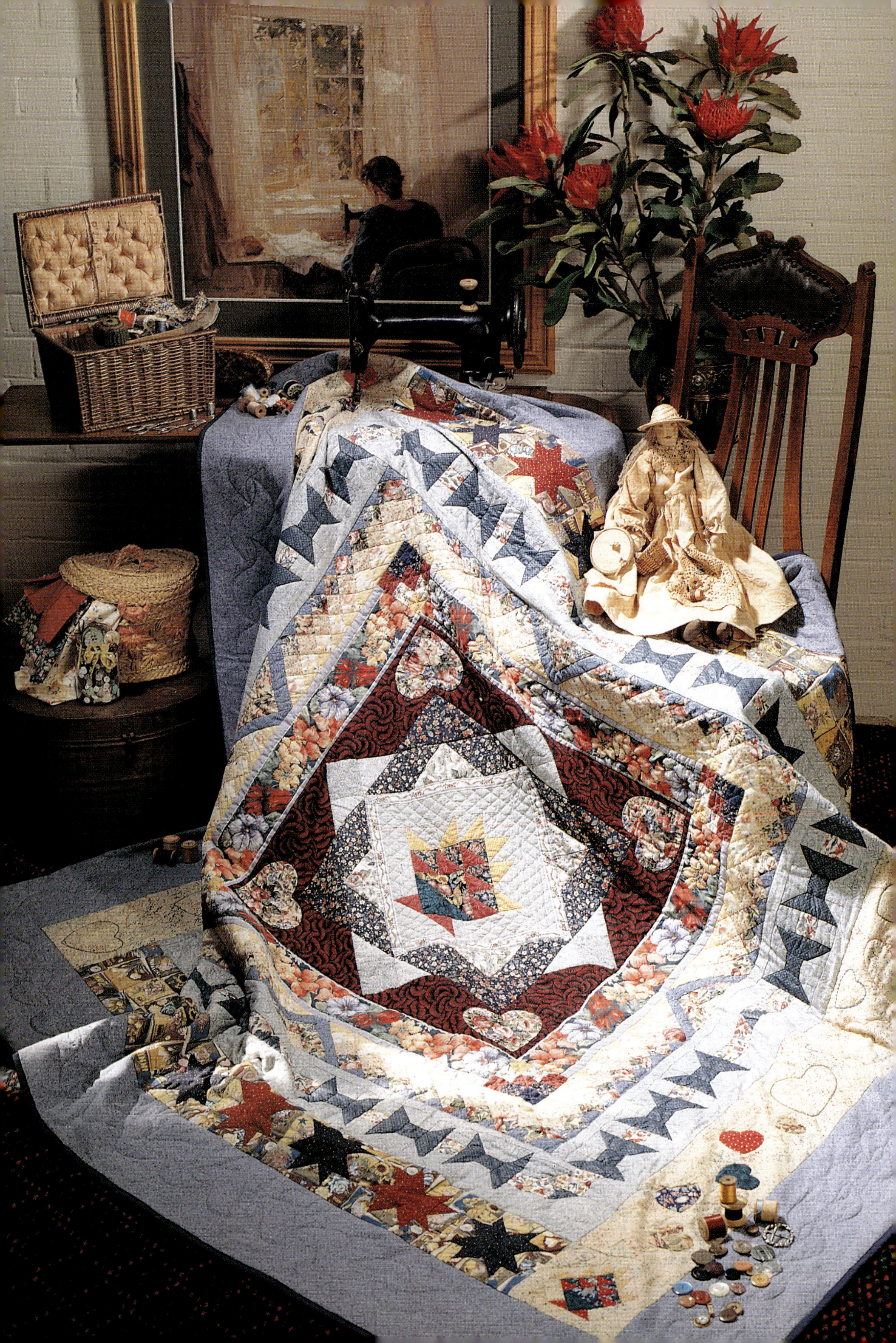

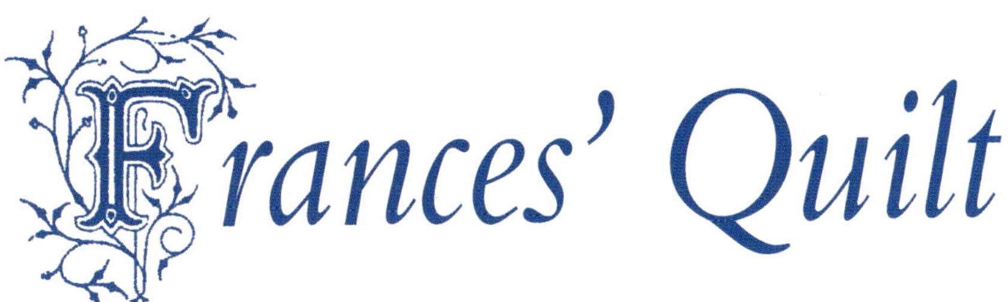

Frances' Quilt

The block at the beginning is a dressed-up traditional basket pattern using strong yellows and clear pinks in a float of powder blue. Squares within squares take us on a journey through ruby reds and French blues with many yellow tones adding sunshine to a truly pretty quilt.

Read the Getting Started and Basic Instructions sections before you begin your quilt.

THE BLOCK

Cut and piece carefully using the block templates and BLOCK DIAGRAM as a guide. Your block should measure 12in x 12in finished when complete.

ROUND ONE

Float a strip cut 1¼in (½in finished) around the block in soft blue floral.

From dark floral fabric cut eight rectangles 7in x 3in.

From light floral fabric cut 16 squares 3in x 3in.

Follow diagram 1 to make four of A and four of B.

Cut four corners 3in x 3in (2½in x 2½in finished) in medium floral fabric and join with A's and B's to complete the round (see Block Diagram).

ROUND TWO

Cut one dark floral square 9in x 9in. Cut into four diagonally (see diagram 2). Cut strips 5½in wide (dark ruby fabric). Sew these to the short sides of the four triangles. Trim off at the lower edge (see diagram 3). Attach these large triangles to the quilt (see Block Diagram).

ROUND THREE

Make four nine-patch blocks for the corners using squares cut 2in x 2in. Choose fabrics in darks and lights. Construct blocks as in diagram 4. Blocks measure 4½in x 4½in finished. Use a large floral fabric to cut connecting strips. Cut four 5in x 26½in (4½in x 26in finished). Join two short sides, then two long sides with the corners to complete the round.

ROUND FOUR

This is a seminole pattern. Choose five fabrics to blend from light to dark and follow diagram 5.

Make a triangular section (see diagram 6) using three seminole fabrics and hand stitch into position where the seminole pattern joins at mid point (see photographs).

ROUND FIVE

Snappy dark bows are strung together on a soft floral ribbon. Follow diagram 7 for bows, diagram 8 for the corner and diagram 9 for connecting strips.

Bow Blocks (make 24)

For each bow cut:

Two rectangles 5in x 2in (dark blue fabric)

One square 2in x 2in (dark blue fabric)

Six squares 2in x 2in (background fabric).

Corner sections (make four)

In background fabric cut:

1½in strips. Float these on the outside of the linked bows (1in finished). Cut float strip 1¼in and sew on inner side of linked bows (½in finished).

ROUND SIX

Make 10 stars – five dark red and five dark blue. Use construction method in diagram 3, Margaret's quilt, with the following new cutting sizes:

A. Cut one 3½in x 3½in (star fabric)

B. Cut four 3½in x 2½in (background fabric)

C. Cut four 2½in x 2½in (background fabric)

D. Cut eight 2in x 2in (star fabric)

Star block is 7in x 7in finished.

For the upper side join together three red and two blue stars alternatively. Cut 7½in strip of background fabric and join with stars to complete the side (stars are set to the left). For the lower side join three blue and two red stars alternatively. Cut 7½in strip of background fabric and join with stars to complete the side (stars are set to the right). See photographs.

ROUND SEVEN

Cut float strips 7½in wide in pale background fabric. Use templates to make hearts in various sizes. Appliqué as shown in photographs.

Frances' quilt has an extra border in solid blue cut 8in wide (7½in finished) on all four sides. This makes it a suitable size for a bed. A continuous quilting design would look attractive on this border.

FINISHED SIZE

83in x 83in (210cm x 210cm)

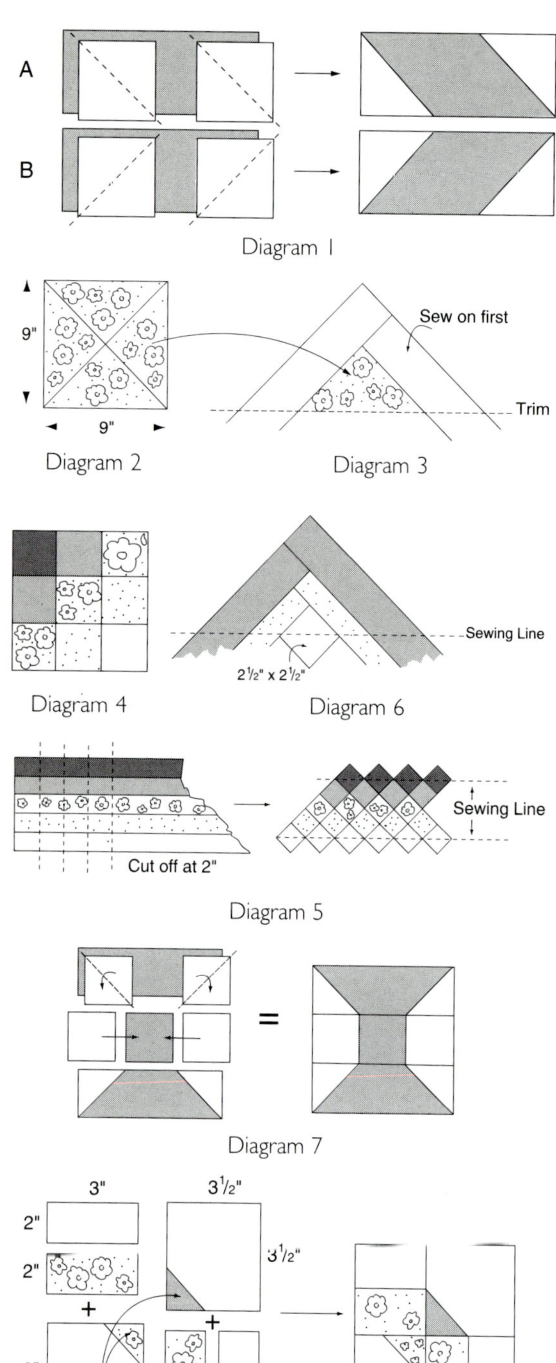

Diagram 1
Diagram 2
Diagram 3
Diagram 4
Diagram 6
Diagram 5
Diagram 7
Diagram 8
Diagram 9

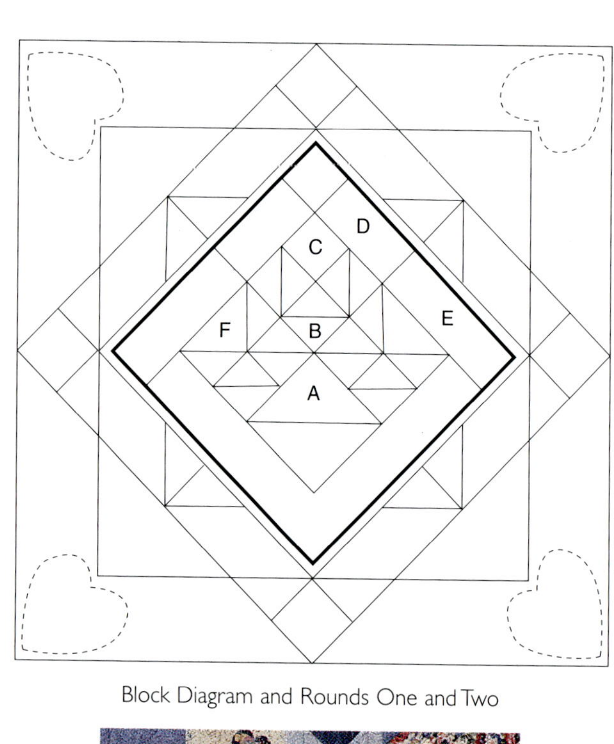

Block Diagram and Rounds One and Two

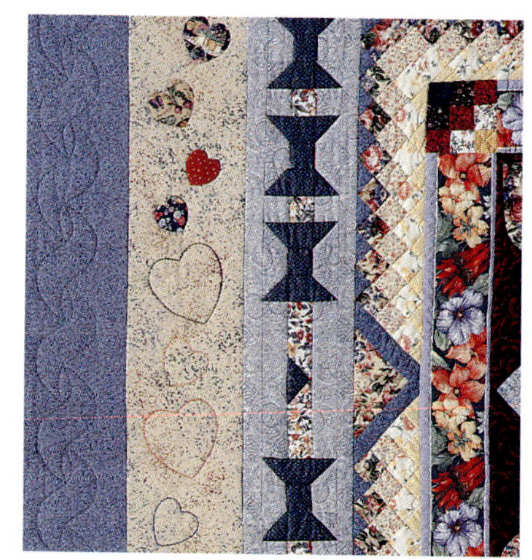

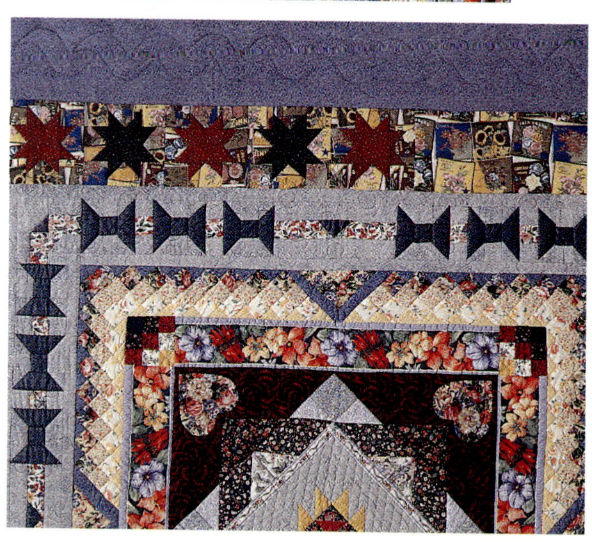

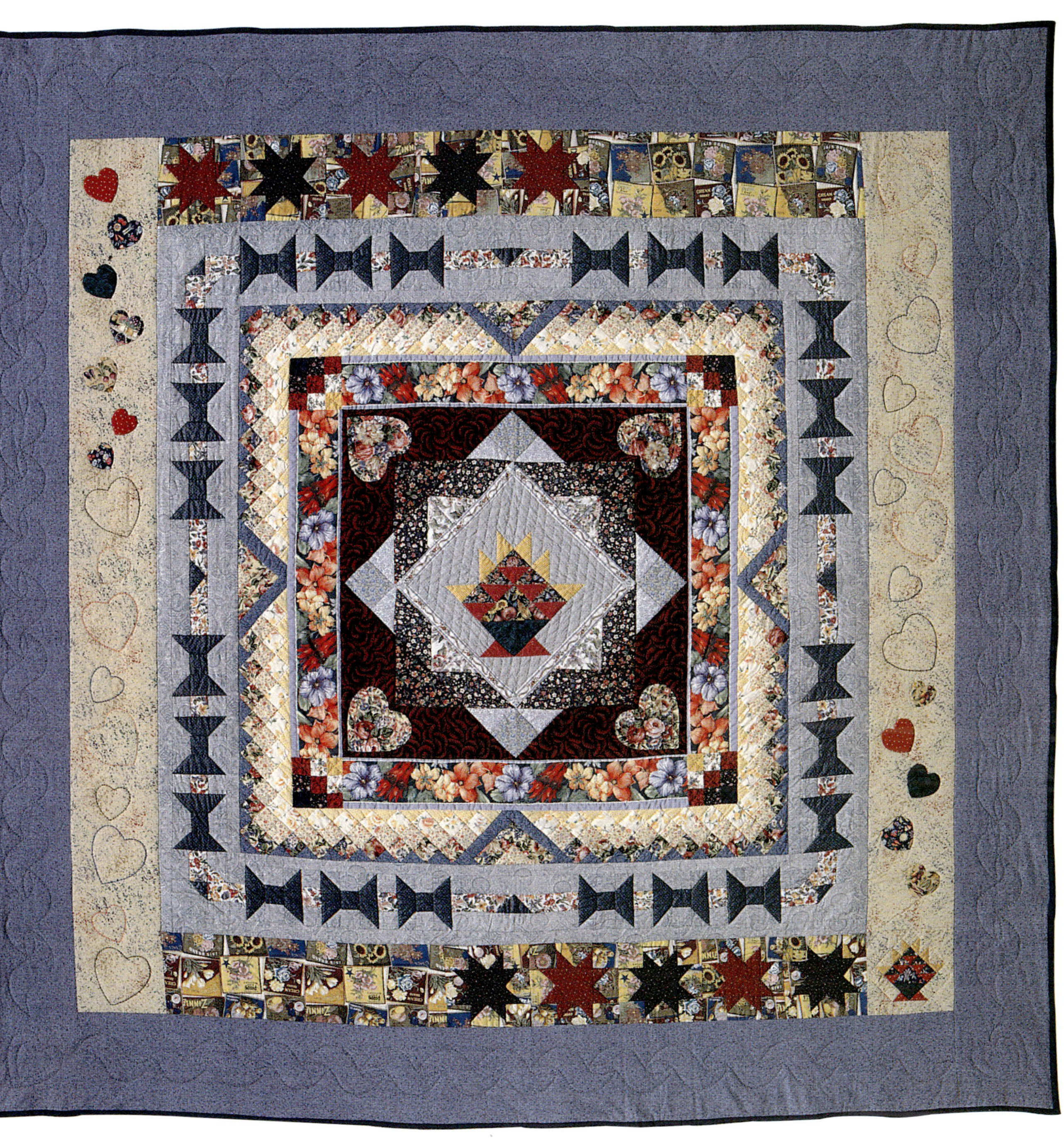

Frances Morris

Frances began quilting 14 years ago, making her first quilt for her son. In recent years she has enjoyed the group's support. Her other love is making bears and cloth dolls, joining the Hello Dollies Newcastle group at their meetings.

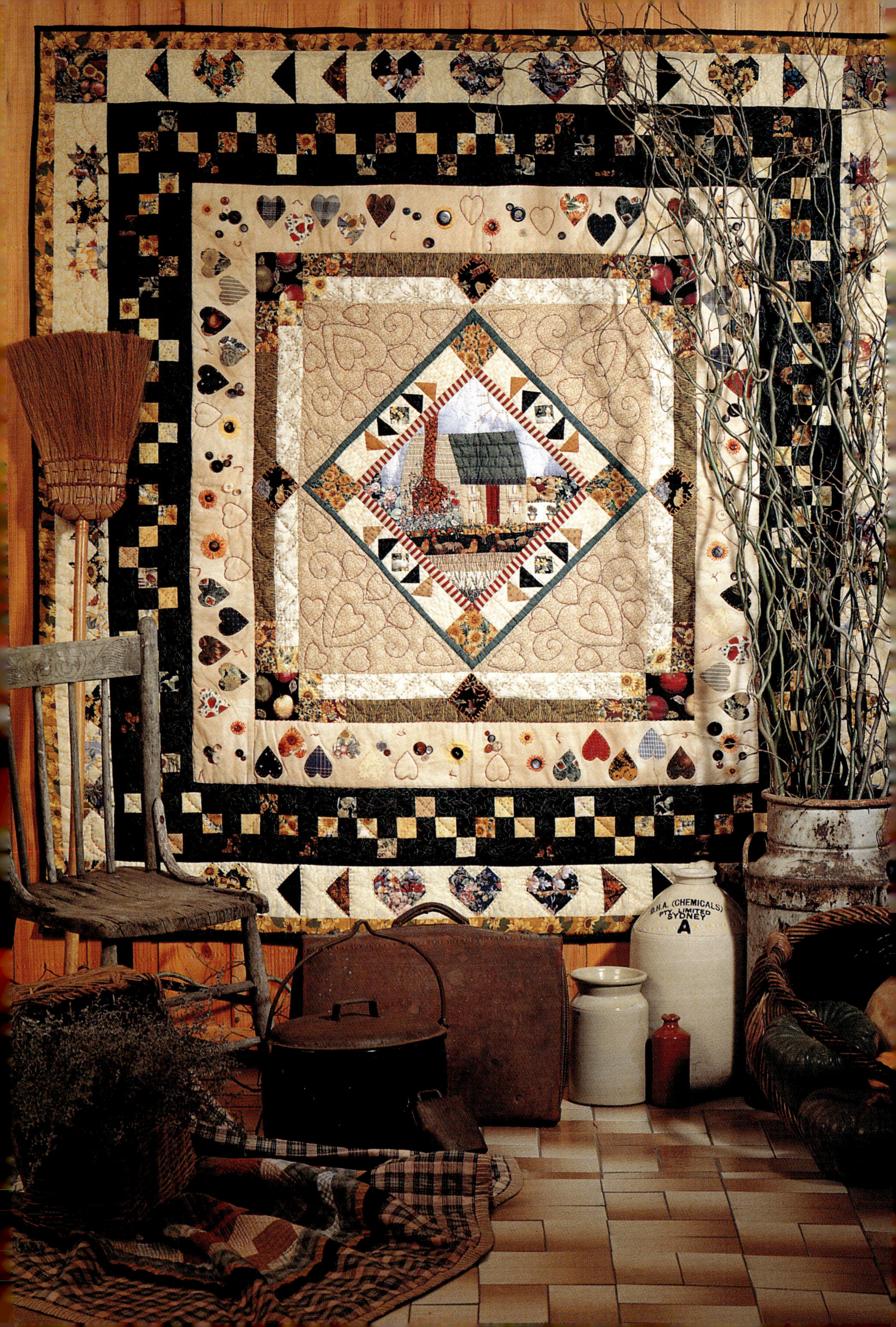
B.H.A. (CHEMICALS)
PTY. LIMITED
SYDNEY
A

Lizzie's Quilt

The block at the beginning features a charming country cottage surrounded by rambling gardens, where hens gather and a scarecrow stands watch. The rounds continue with simple patterns in rich greens and sunflower yellows. The atmosphere is about golden days, long warm afternoons and endless hours quilting around the log fire.

Read the Getting Started and Basic Instructions sections before you begin your quilt.

THE BLOCK

Cut and piece carefully using the block templates and the BLOCK DIAGRAM as a guide. Appliqué the chimney into position to complete the block. Your block should measure 12in x 12in finished when complete.

ROUND ONE

Cut four corner squares 3in x 3in (2½in x 2½in finished). For connecting strips, cut four cream 2½in x 12½in and four striped 1¼in x 12½in finished. Sew one cream and one striped fabric strip together. Make four of these sets. Sew with striped side towards the block on two opposite sides. Add the corners for the long sides. Cut float strip 1¼in wide (½in finished) and sew to all sides. Appliqué squares on point and flying geese triangles to cream fabric using templates on pattern sheet. See block diagram.

ROUND TWO

Cut four large triangles, see diagram 1. You may wish to stabilise the bias edges with a row of stitching to prevent stretching. Attach the triangles by the long edge to the four sides of Round One (see photographs).

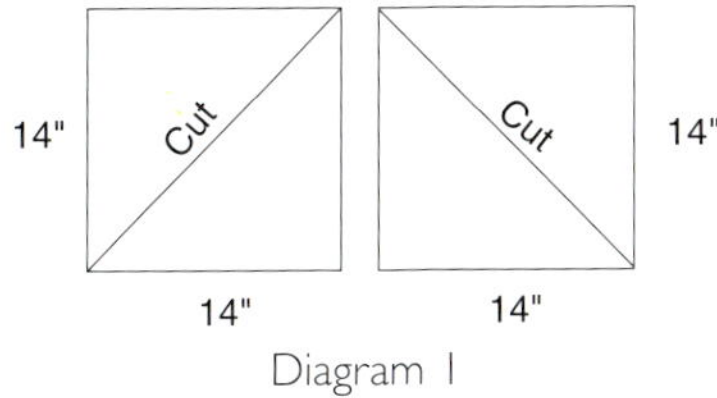

Diagram 1

ROUND THREE

Cut four corner squares 4in x 4in (3½in x 3½in finished). Connecting strips need three colour-wash squares at each end (cut 2¼in x 2¼in). Cut strips 2¼in wide (inner strip 19½in long and outer strip 23in long) to join with colour-wash squares and complete the round, checking photographs for placement.

Optional addition: Four extra squares at mid point are cut 3in x 3in. Press under ¼in allowance all around and use Perlé cotton to blanket stitch in position when all rounds are complete.

ROUND FOUR

This border uses tea-dyed cream homespun. Dye, dry and press fabric before you begin cutting. Cut two strips 5½in x 33½in for two opposite sides and two strips 5½in x 43½in for the two long sides. Sew these to your quilt. Decorate with hearts applied with light-weight fusible webbing (template supplied) and old buttons in various sizes.

ROUND FIVE

Choose a dark background fabric with sunny bright floral accents to make nine-patch blocks. You will need 24 of diagram 2 and 20 of diagram 3. The squares are cut 2in x 2in (1½in x 1½in finished) sewn blocks measure 5in x 5in (4½in x 4½in finished).

Use the dark background fabric to float strips on inner and outer edges of joined nine-patch blocks. Cut inner strips 1½in wide (1in finished) and outer strips 1¼in wide (½in finished).

Nine patch blocks

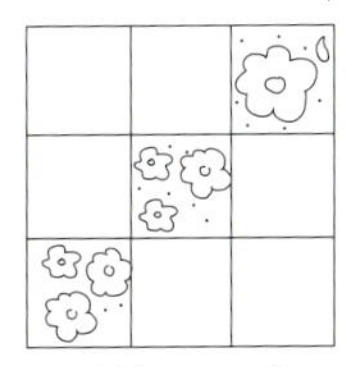
Diagram 2

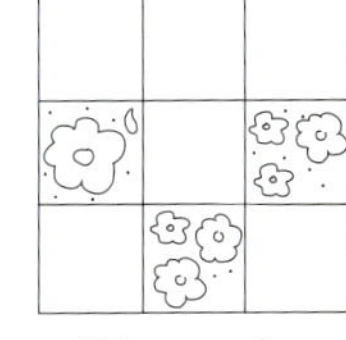
Diagram 3

ROUND SIX

Make two opposite sides of stars. Follow diagram 3 Margaret's Quilt, with these new cutting sizes:

A. Cut one 2½in x 2½in (star fabric)
B. Cut four 2½in x 1½in (background fabric)
C. Cut four 1½in x 1½in (background fabric)
D. Cut eight 1½in x 1½in (star fabric).

Twelve stars will fit each side – you may make less and space them apart with background fabric.

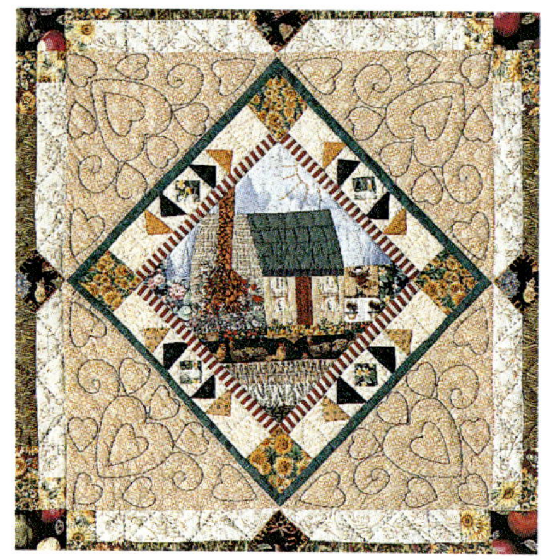

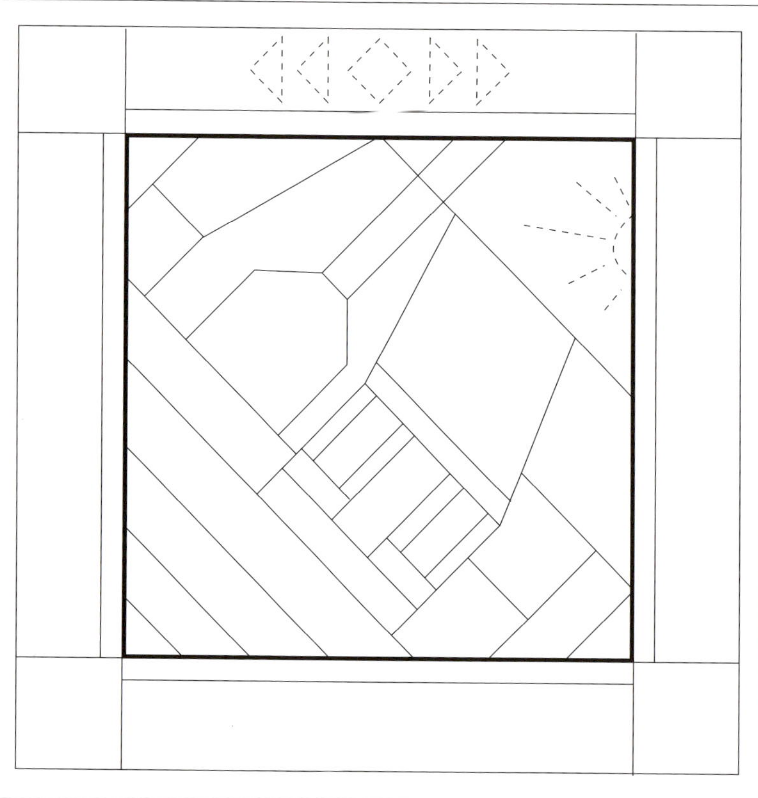

Block Diagram and Round One

ROUND SEVEN

A combination of hearts and flying geese run along the top and lower edges of the quilt in a background of antique cream with four 'sunflower' fabric corners cut $4\frac{1}{2}$in x $4\frac{1}{2}$in (4in x 4in finished). Make ten hearts using the pattern in diagram 4, round 6 and 7 Margaret's Quilt.

Flying Geese (make 12)

Rectangles are cut $2\frac{1}{2}$in x $4\frac{1}{2}$in (accent colour). Corners for folded out triangles are cut $2\frac{1}{2}$in x $2\frac{1}{2}$in see diagram 4.

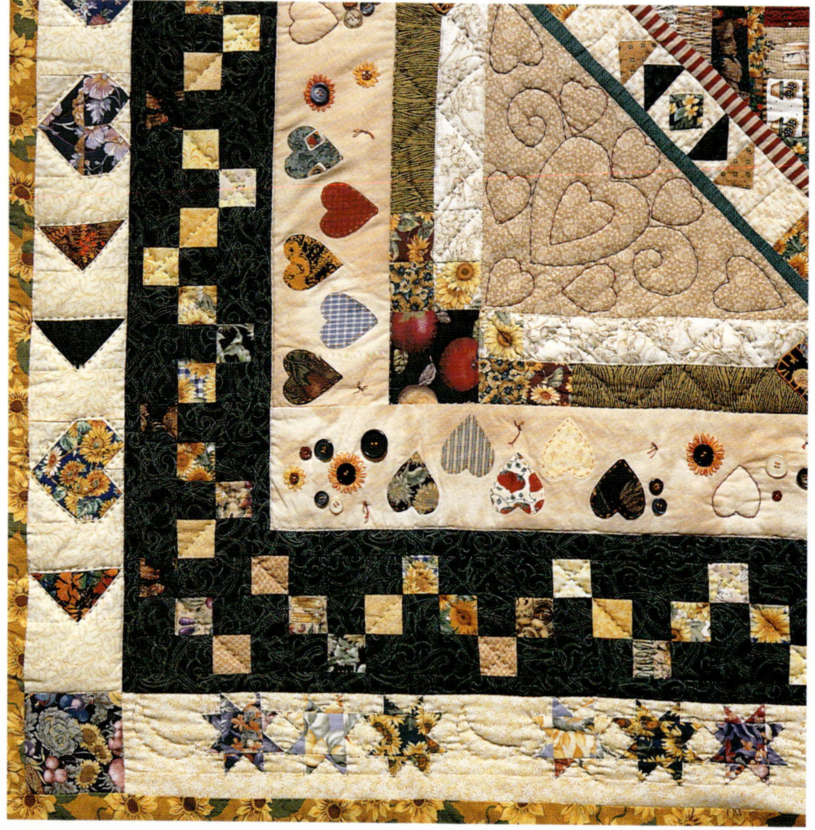

i)

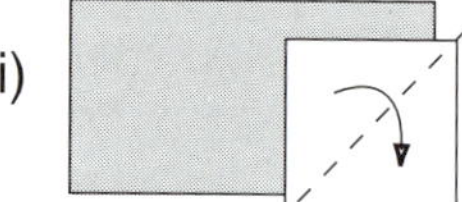

ii)

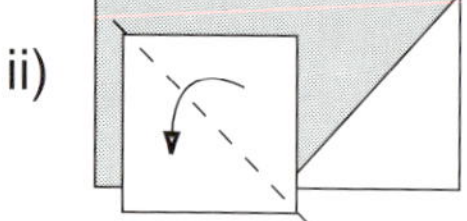

iii)

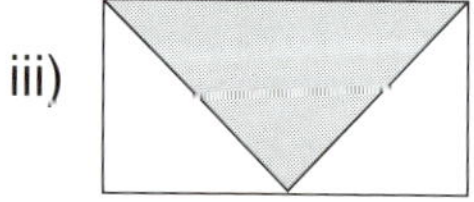

Diagram 4

Join hearts and flying geese with background fabric between (see photographs), adding in the sunflower corners matching seams carefully. A large-scale sunflower fabric cut 2in wide ($1\frac{1}{2}$in finished) surrounds the quilt.

FINISHED SIZE

64in x 64in (163cm x 163cm)

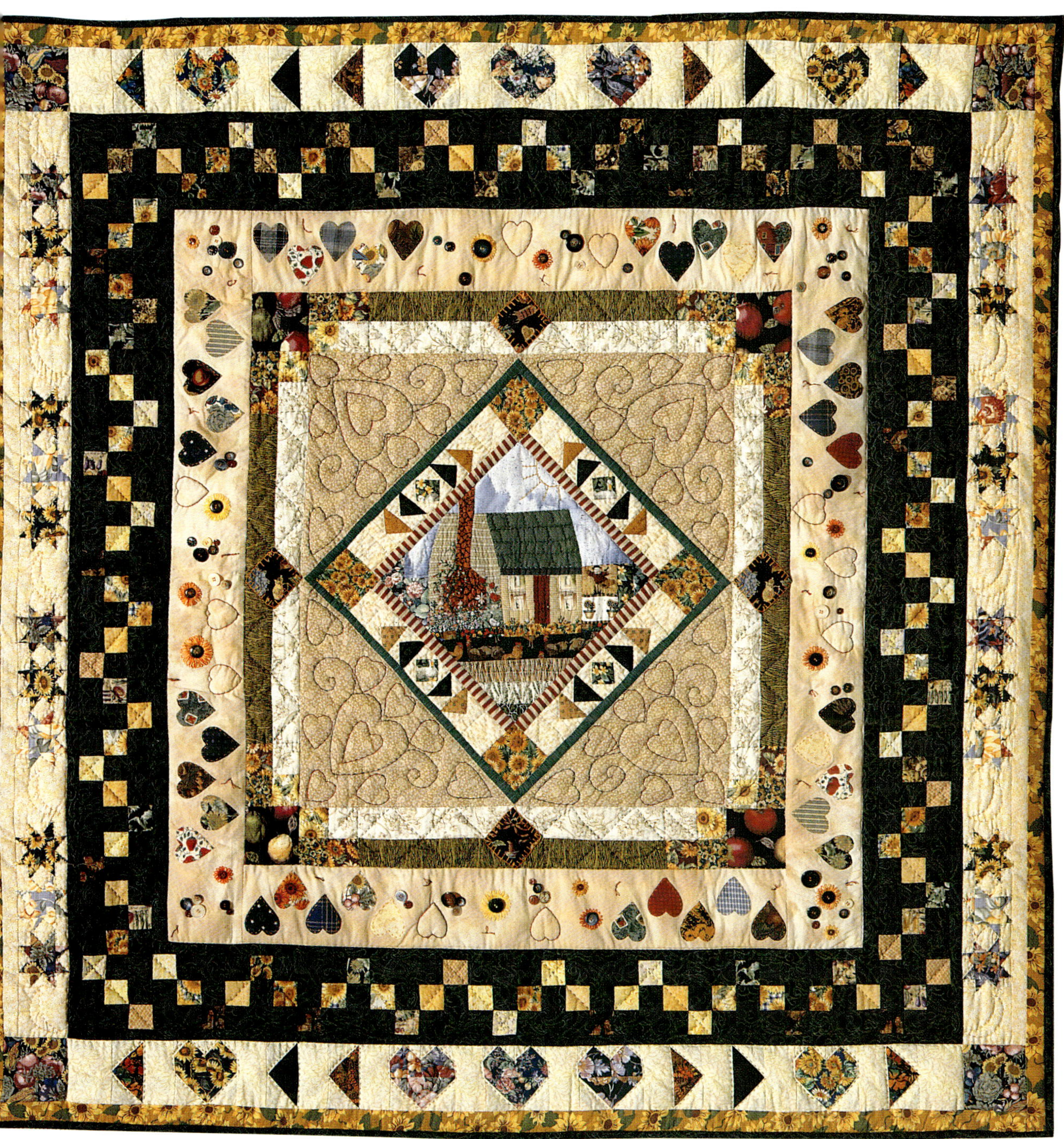

Lizzie Grabham

Lizzie found time for quilting about two years ago when her young family all reached school age. Her special interest is in 'country' look quilts and fabrics and her wish is for more hours in the day to play with the stash.

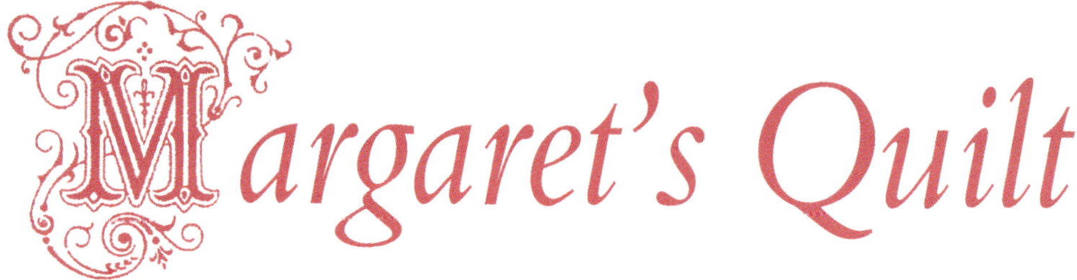

Margaret's Quilt

The block at the beginning is a neat geometric design with an interesting range of colours and prints. The impression is of the jewel-like beauty of gemstones and the rounds following burst into a kaleidoscope of amethyst, jade, ruby and opal set occasionally with smart black accents.

Read the Getting Started and Basic Instructions sections before you begin your quilt.

THE BLOCK

Cut and piece carefully using the block templates and the BLOCK DIAGRAM as a guide. Your block should measure 12in x 12in finished when complete.

ROUND ONE

This round uses the small and the medium triangle templates from the block. Cut and piece, following the block diagram guide. Cut float strips 1½in wide (1in finished) and sew onto four sides to complete the round.

ROUND TWO

Cut four large triangles (see diagram 1). You may wish to stabilise the bias edges with a row of stitching to prevent stretching. Attach the triangles by the long edge to the four sides of Round One (see photograph).

Cut four float strips 1¼in (½in finished) in a contrast fabric and sew onto four sides.

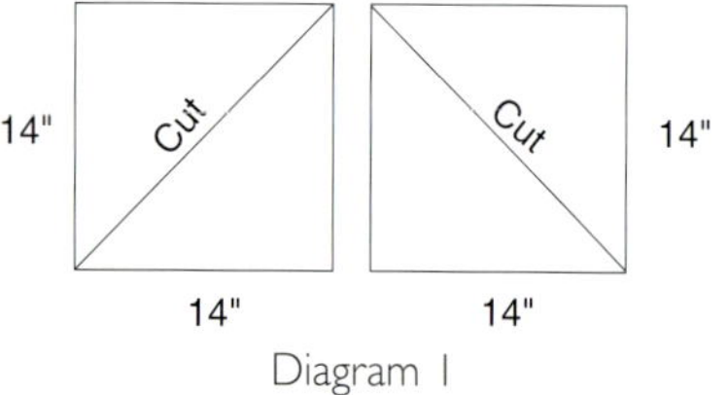

Diagram 1

ROUND THREE

Cut four 3½in x 3½in squares for corners (3in x 3in finished).

Cut four connecting strips 3½in x 27in (3in x 26½in finished).

Sew two connecting strips to the quilt on opposite sides. Join two squares on each end of the remaining two connecting strips. Sew to the long sides of the quilt, matching seams at the corners.

ROUND FOUR
The corners

Cut four squares 3½in x 3½in. Add a float (cut 1in wide) around all sides of the squares.

The connecting strips

These are made with two fabrics. It is suggested the wider strip is much paler than the narrow strip. Cut the wide strips 4in x 33in and narrow strips 1¼in x 33in. Join the narrow strip to the wide strip. Join corners and connecting strips to your quilt. Add two float strips to complete the round, the first one in light, bright fabric cut 2in wide (1½in finished) and the second strip in medium coloured fabric cut 1¼in (½in finished).

ROUND FIVE

Make 12 nine-patch blocks (see diagram 2). Squares are cut 1½in x 1½in. Use a selection of jewel coloured fabrics with black fabric repeated in all blocks.

The connecting strips are cut 1½in wide in black and jewel colours. Sew one black strip on either side of one jewel strip. Assemble nine-patch squares and connecting sections around your quilt (see photographs) to complete Round Five.

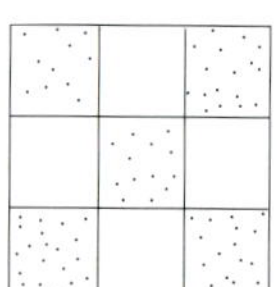

Nine-patch block

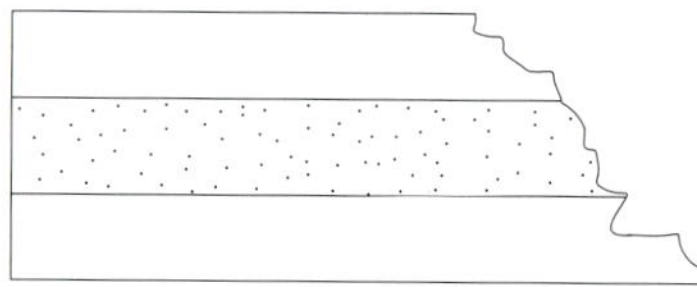

Connecting strips

Diagram 2

ROUND SIX AND SEVEN

For this round, stars and hearts come together with one fabric repeated throughout the background. Make your stars and hearts using diagram 3 and diagram 4. Cut float strips to set them apart as shown in the photograph.

Star Block (make 12):

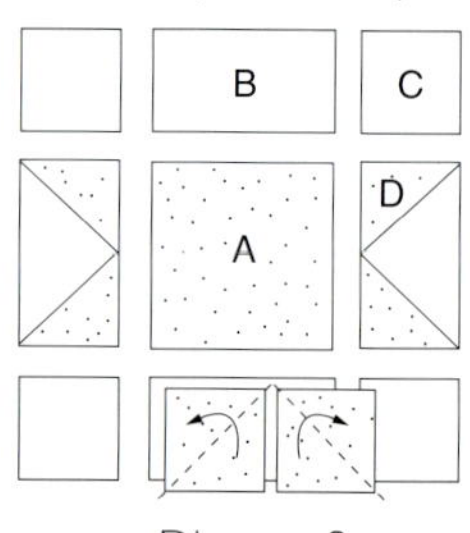

Diagram 3

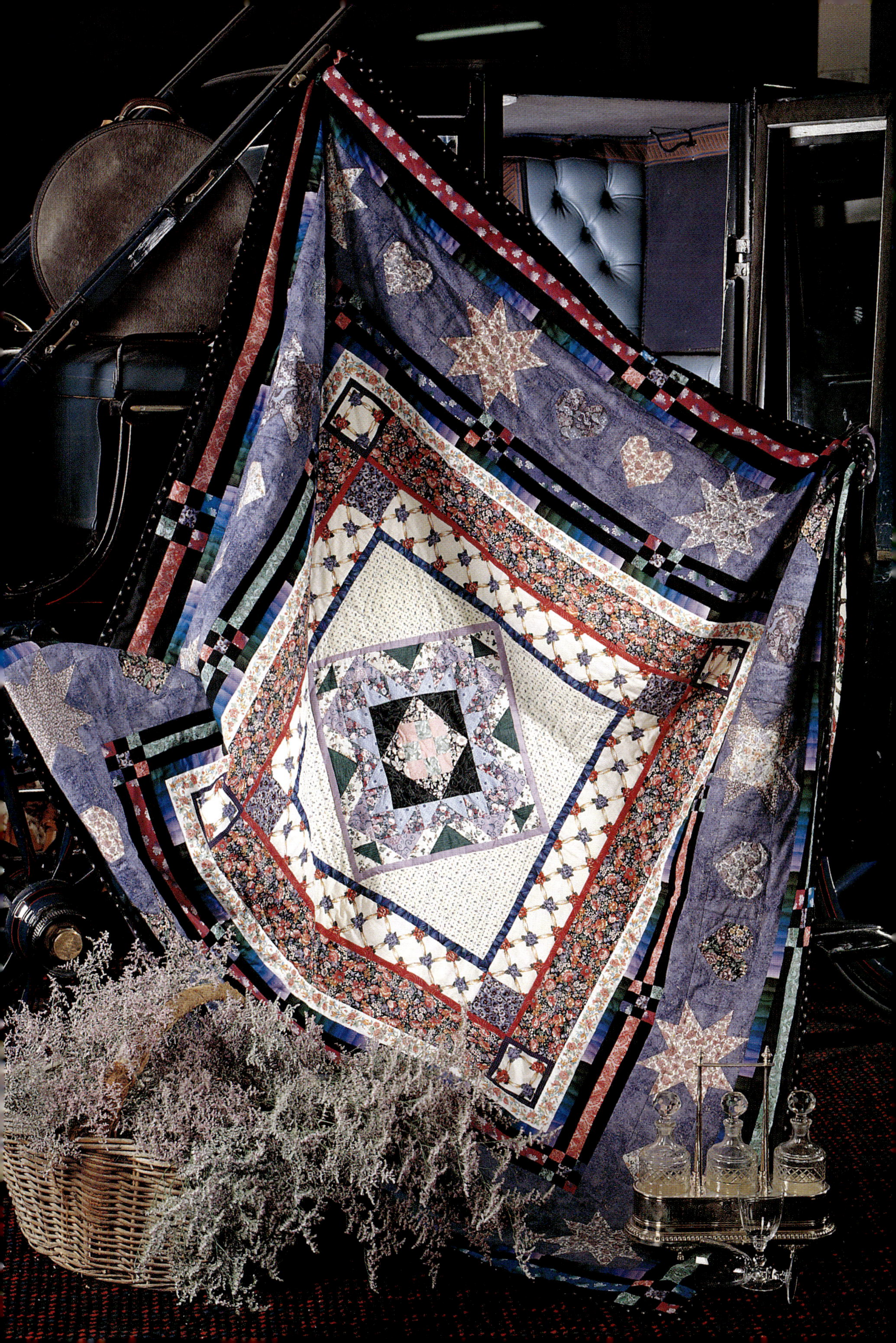

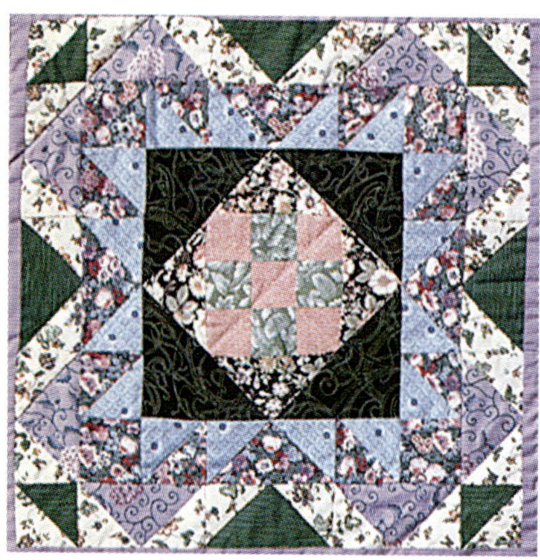

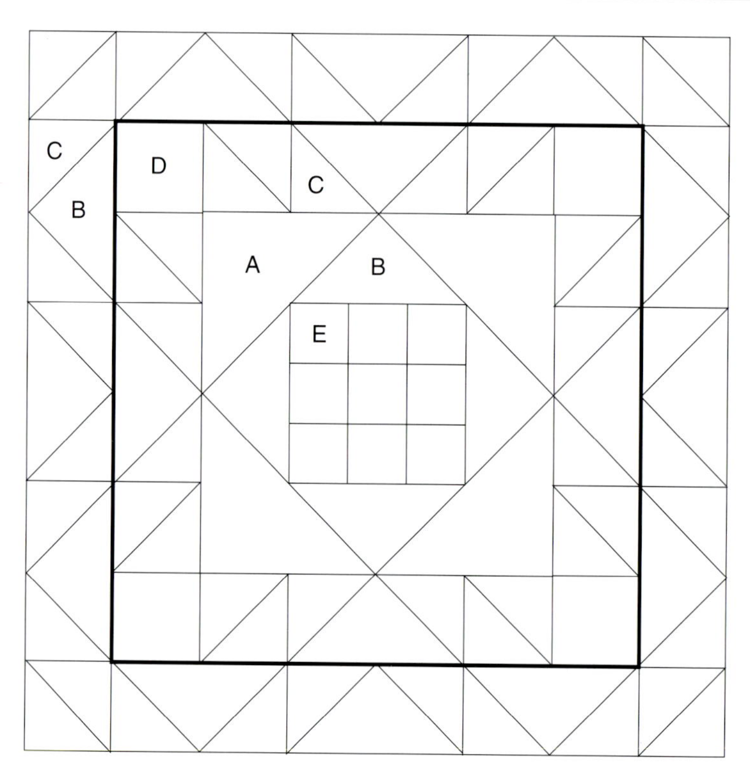

Block Diagram and Round One

Cutting sizes for stars

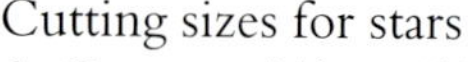

A. Cut one 4½in x 4½in (star fabric)
B. Cut four 4½in x 2½in (background fabric)
C. Cut four 2½in x 2½in (background fabric)
D. Cut eight 2½in x 2½in (star fabric).

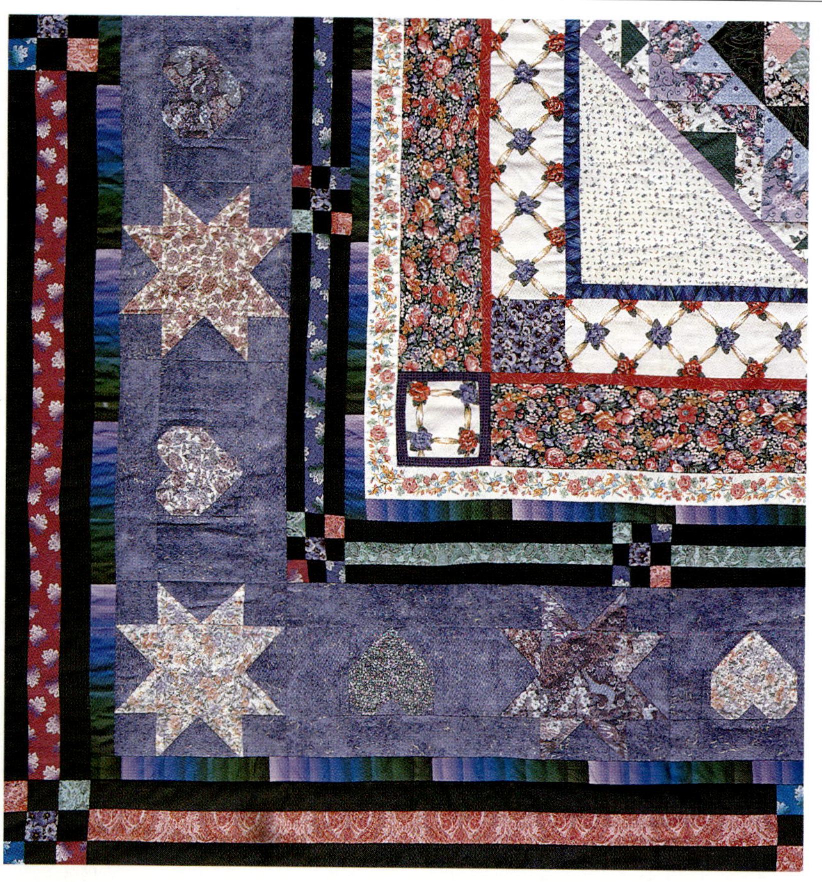

Heart Block (make 16)

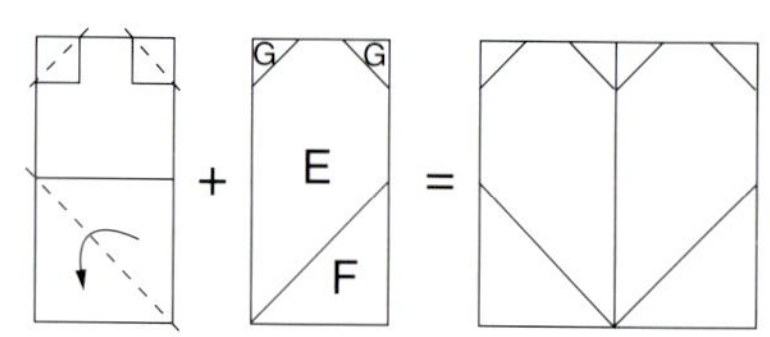

Diagram 4

Cutting sizes for hearts:
E. Cut two 4½in x 2½in (heart fabric)
F. Cut two 2½in x 2½in (background fabric)
G. Cut four 1¼in x 1¼in (background fabric).

One final round has been added – an enlarged version of Round Five. You may wish to finish your quilt in this way. If you do, choose similar colours with black again as the accent fabric.

FINISHED SIZE
76½in x 76½in (194cm x 194cm)

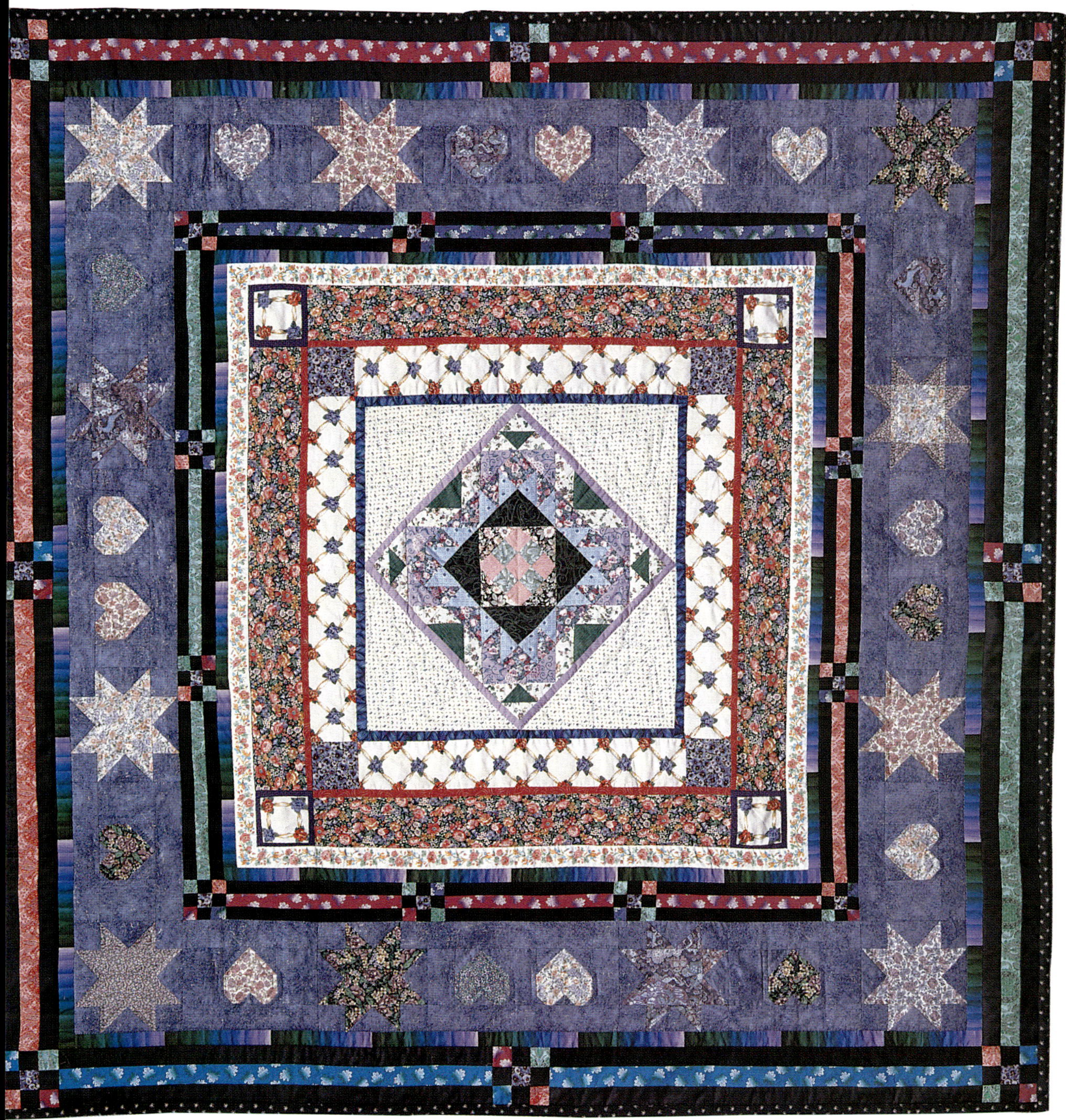

Margaret Bryden

Margaret's interest in quilting developed as she watched her friend Yan's passion for the craft. Nine years ago she plunged in the deep end – filling the sewing room with books, magazines and fabric. She makes many quilts for family and friends.

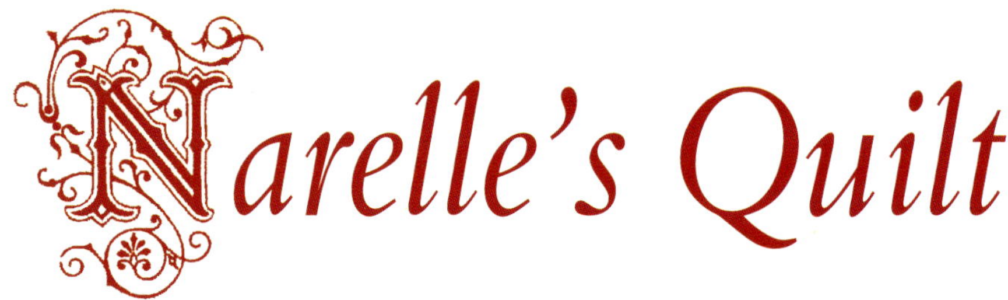

Narelle's Quilt

The block at the beginning focuses on a little country home with the proud owner peeping from the front window. Warm tones set the mood for a great outdoor life filled with sunshine, starlight, sunflowers and a deep love for all that is down-on-the-farm.

Read the Getting Started and Basic Instructions sections before you begin your quilt.

THE BLOCK

Cut and piece carefully using the block templates and BLOCK DIAGRAM as a guide. Add a float strip (cut 1¼in wide) in a deep accent colour to four sides of the block. Your block should measure 12in x 12in finished when complete.

ROUND ONE

Half square triangles are used in this round. Select fabrics which contrast and make 20 squares (see diagram 1). Note: each set will yield two finished squares.

Cut all squares 4in x 4in. This gives 3in x 3in finished size. Place two contrasting squares right sides together.

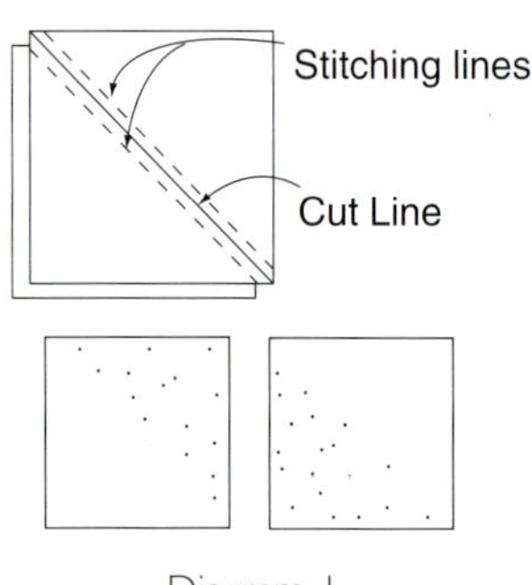

Diagram 1

ROUND TWO

Cut four large triangles (see diagram 2). You may wish to stabilise the bias edges with a row of stitching to prevent stretching. Attach the triangles by the long edge to the four sides of round one, see photographs.

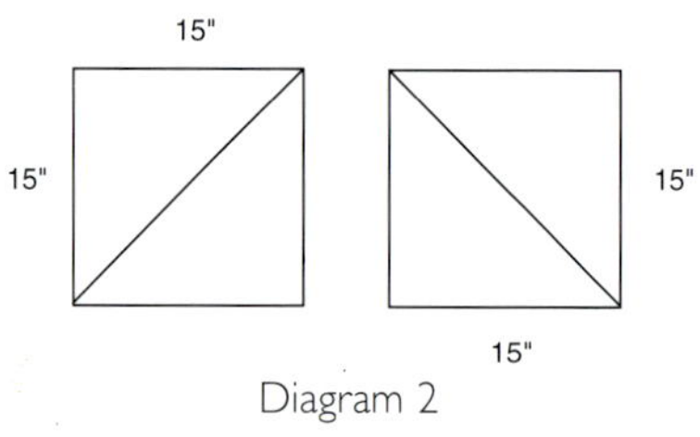

Diagram 2

ROUND THREE

Cut four corner squares in dark accent fabric (country red) 4in x 4in (3½in x 3½in finished). The connecting section between the corners is made with four-patch blocks in black and cream. Cut black and cream strips 2¼in wide, sew together lengthwise and cut across at 2¼in (see diagram 3).

Make 32 four-patch blocks (3½in x 3½in finished). Sew eight together for each opposite side. Sew eight together with corner squares at each end for the other two sides, see photograph.

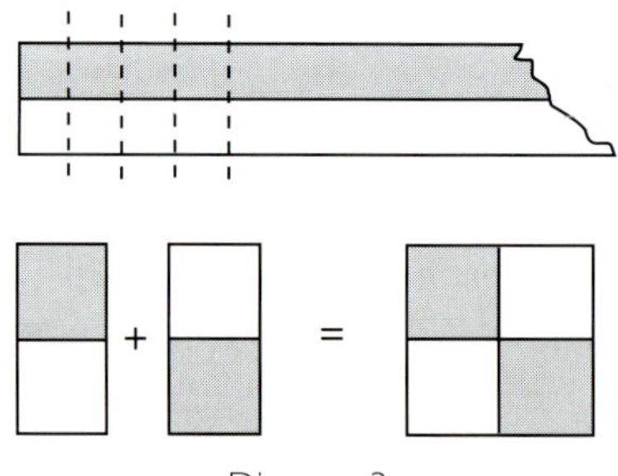

Diagram 3

ROUND FOUR

Make a panorama with farm scene fabric, cloudy sky print and various tones and prints to represent hills and paddocks. Allow 10½in finished for this section, creating a design to suit your fabrics. Narelle's Quilt uses appliqué for the hills and a float strip as part of the border on the top and two sides.

ROUND FIVE

On the lower edge of the quilt only, follow diagram 4 to make the fence. Choose two background fabrics that suggest gardens and one 'rustic' fabric for the post-and-rail fence.

Cut three strips 2½in wide of fence fabric. Cut one strip of each garden fabric 2½in wide. Sew a garden strip either side of one fence strip. Cut off at 4½in sections (eight needed). Cut remaining two fence strips at 6½in lengths (ten needed). Construct fence as in photograph.

You may wish to leave out the rail in the centre section for a gateway, as in Narelle's Quilt. Cut float strip 1¼in wide of garden

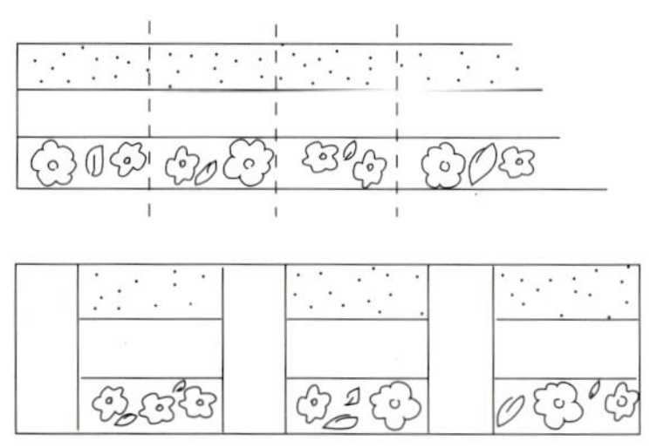

Diagram 4

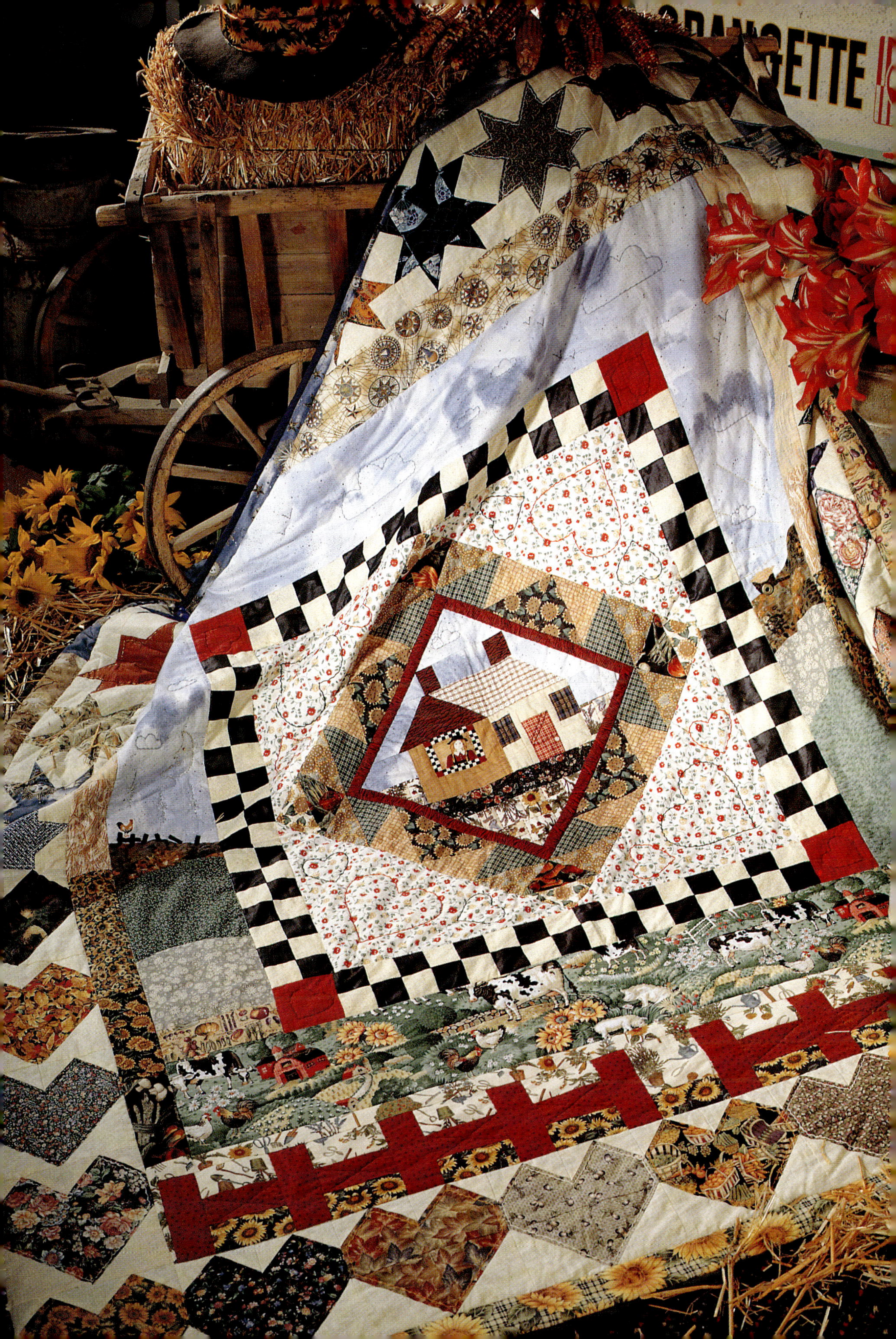

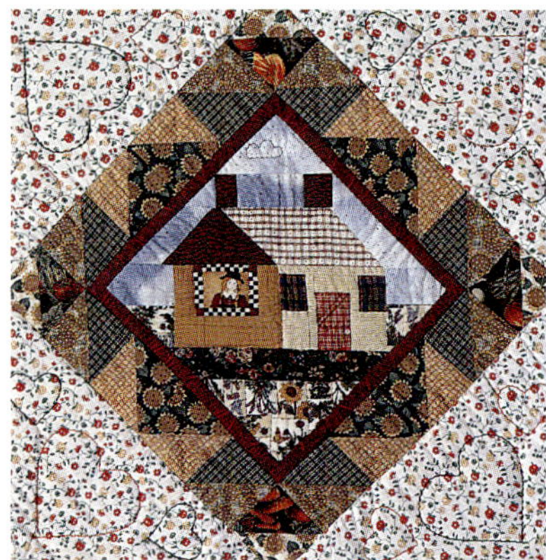

fabric and sew along the top of the fence then attach to the quilt on the lower edge of the farm scene.

ROUND SIX AND SEVEN

A combination of country hearts and stars made from a collection of 'conversation' fabrics, float in a background of antique cream. Use the star pattern in Margaret's quilt, diagram 3. Make eleven full stars, four elongated stars (leave off alternate points) and two half stars. This completes the upper section of the round (see photographs).

Country hearts (make 17)

For each heart:

Cut two squares 4½in x 4½in and one square 5in x 5in (heart fabric).

Cut one square 5in x 5in and four squares 2½in x 2½in (background fabric).

Use the large squares to make the lower sections of the heart (see diagram 1) and follow diagram 5 to complete the heart.

Use conversation fabrics to frame the stars and hearts. On Narelle's Quilt this float strip is cut 3in wide.

FINISHED SIZE

76in x 82in (193cm x 208cm)

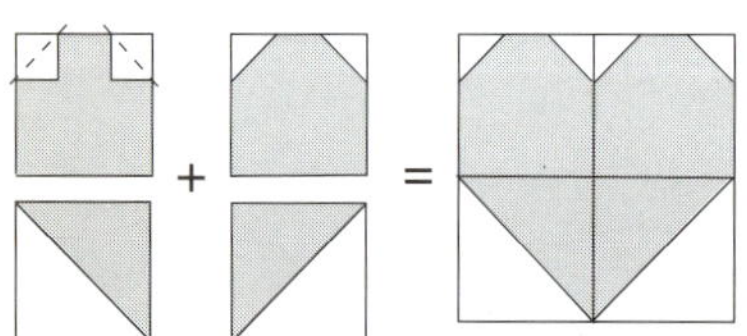

Diagram 5

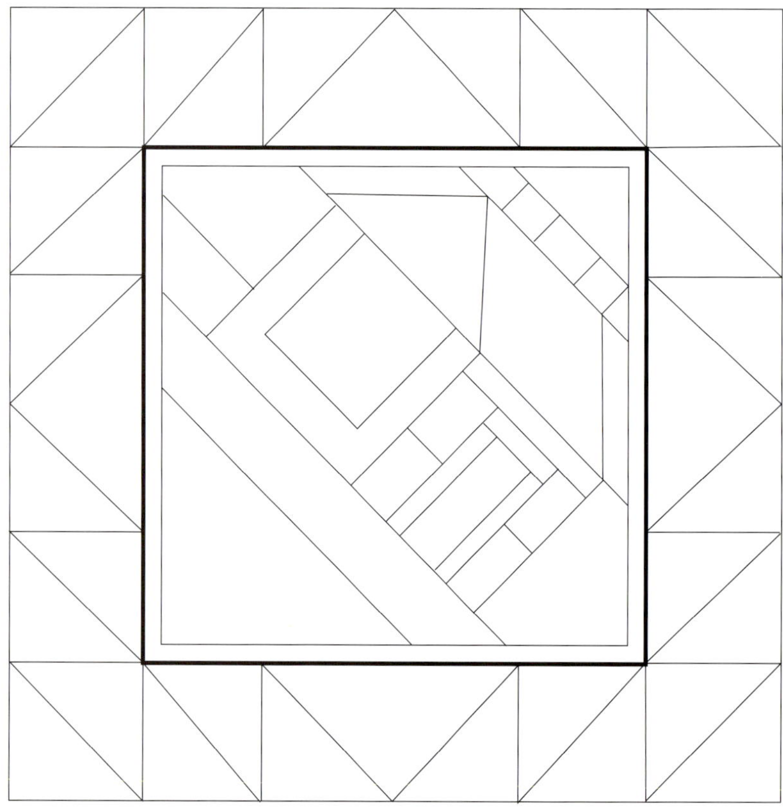

Block Diagram and Round One

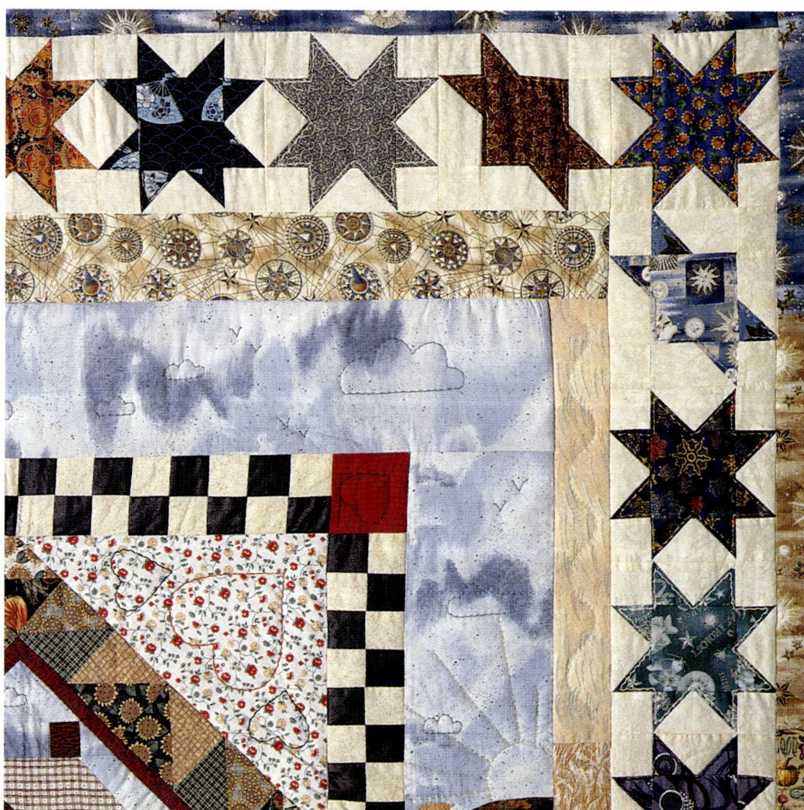

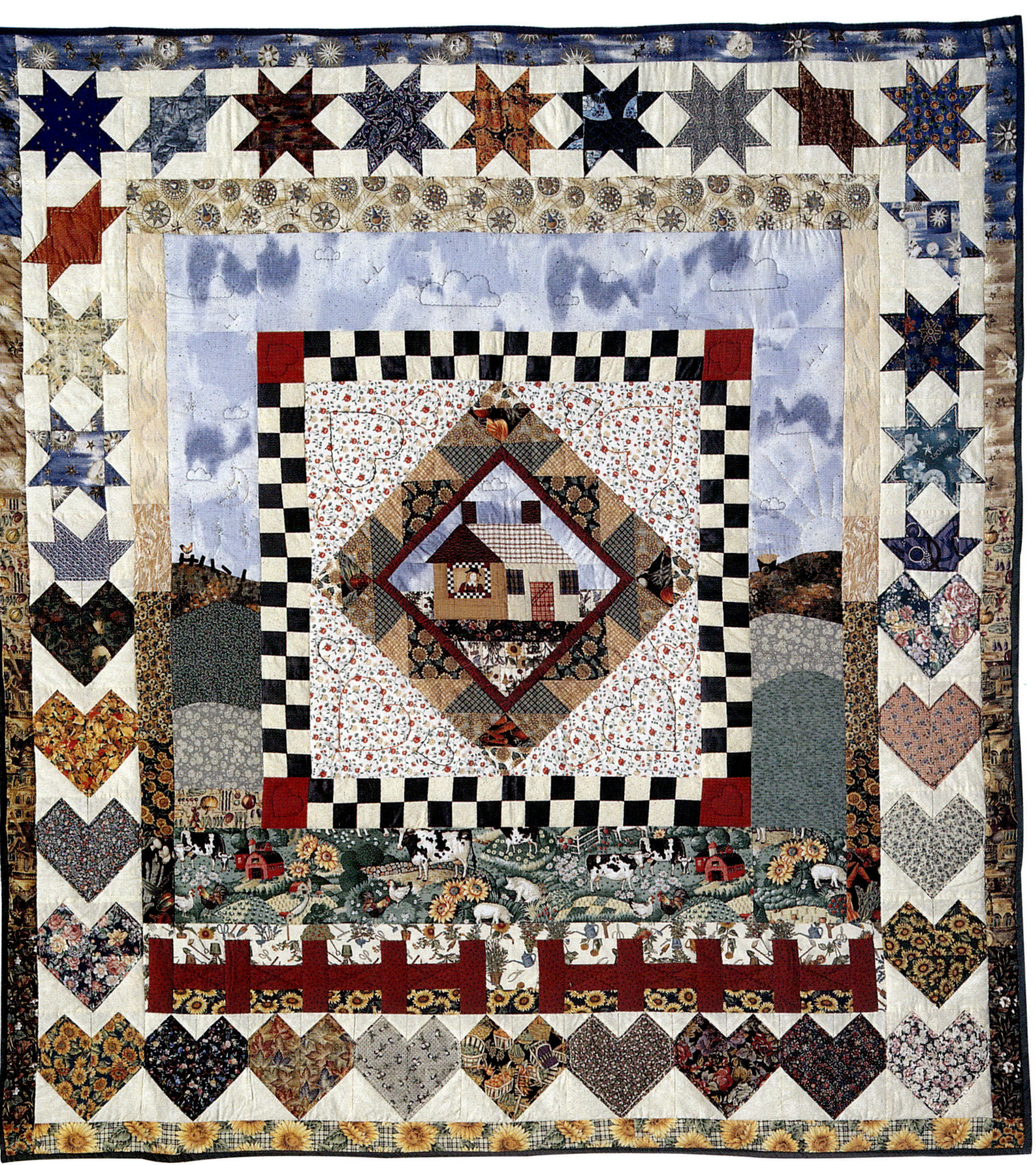

Narelle Elloy

Narelle is the newest member of the group and being a young mum, quilting gives her a much needed escape. Only two years into her quilt journey, she has an impressive collection of quilts – mostly made during her one free night of the week. 'Too busy' is not an excuse for Narelle.

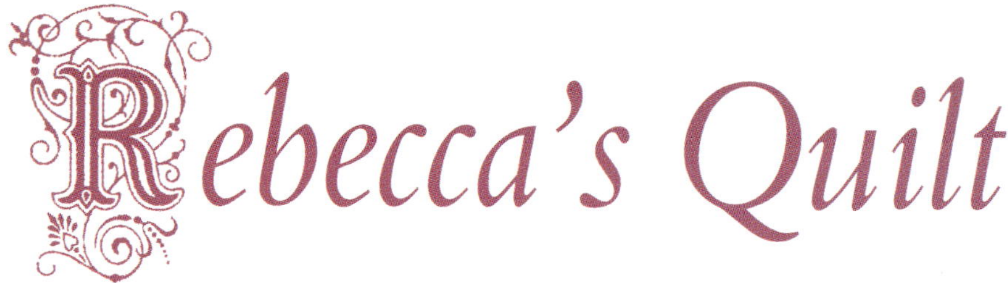

Rebecca's Quilt

The block at the beginning is a rich concentration of deep country green, burgundy and old gold. The theme is set for a story about apple country complete with orchards, cottages, apple trees and baskets of juicy ripe fruit – certainly a quilt to bring joy to a country heart.

Read the Getting Started and Basic Instructions sections before you begin your quilt.

THE BLOCK

Cut and piece carefully using the block templates and BLOCK DIAGRAM as a guide. Your block should measure 12in x 12in finished when complete.

ROUND ONE

Cut a float strip 1¼in wide (½in finished) in medium colour and sew around your block. Use templates included to cut and assemble the pieced section of this round (see block diagram). Remember to add seam allowances to templates. Cut another float strip 1¼in wide (½in finished) in dark colour to sew to outer edge of this round.

ROUND TWO

Follow instructions in diagram 1 Margaret's Quilt for the four large triangles. The float strip for Rebecca's quilt is cut 2in wide.

ROUND THREE

Cut 40 squares 2½in x 2½in in a range of medium tones. Also cut 88 squares 2½in x 2½in in background fabric. Sew into sets shown in diagram 1 (i and ii). Following the photographs sew the sets around the quilt along the sewing line indicated in diagram 1 (iii). Do not stretch your border. Sew on 2in cut (1½in finished) light floral float strip.

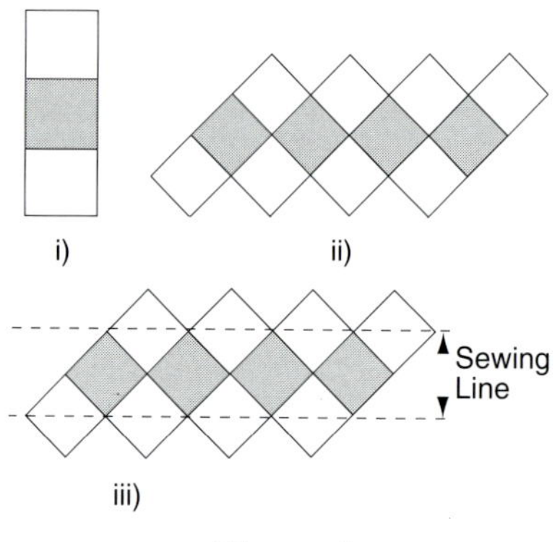

Diagram 1

ROUND FOUR

Cut float strips for this round. The first strip is cut 3in wide (2½in finished). The second strip is cut 1¼in wide (½in finished) in small dark floral. The third strip is cut 4½in wide (4in finished) in a dark large-scale floral.

ROUND FIVE

Here is an opportunity to use some printed landscape fabric. The border scene on Rebecca's quilt measures 9in wide finished. You may need to adjust this section in width to suit the fabric you have chosen. Follow diagrams 2, 3 and 4 for cottages, trees and apple baskets. Enlarge these patterns and place in a pleasing design to best suit the landscape fabrics.

Cottage block (diagram 2)

Draw pattern to full scale, make templates and allow seams when cutting. Adjust the scale if necessary to suit your fabrics.

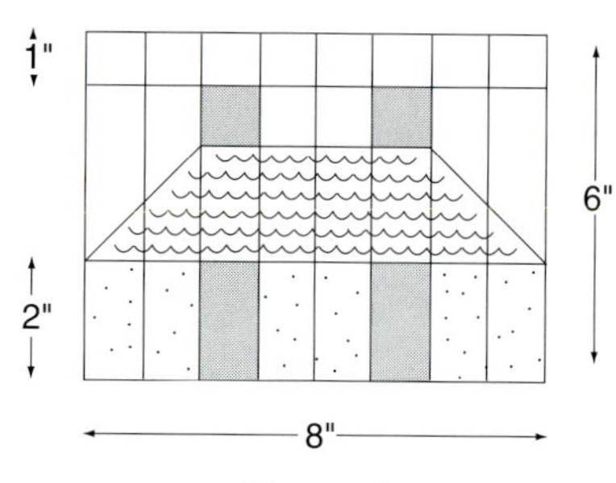

Diagram 2

Trees (diagram 3)

Cut squares in tree fabric 4in x 4in and 3in x 3in.

Add background corners (four for each) cut 1¼in x 1¼in.

Cut trunks from 1in strips and float in background fabric.

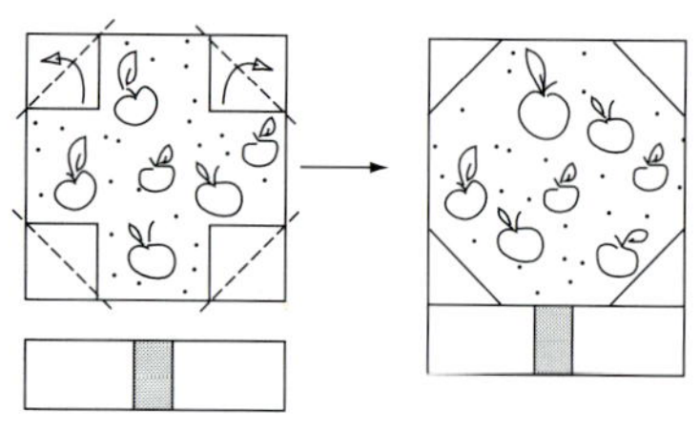

Diagram 3

Basket block (diagram 4)

Make half square triangles (see Narelle's quilt, diagram 1 Round One) in two sizes: large cut

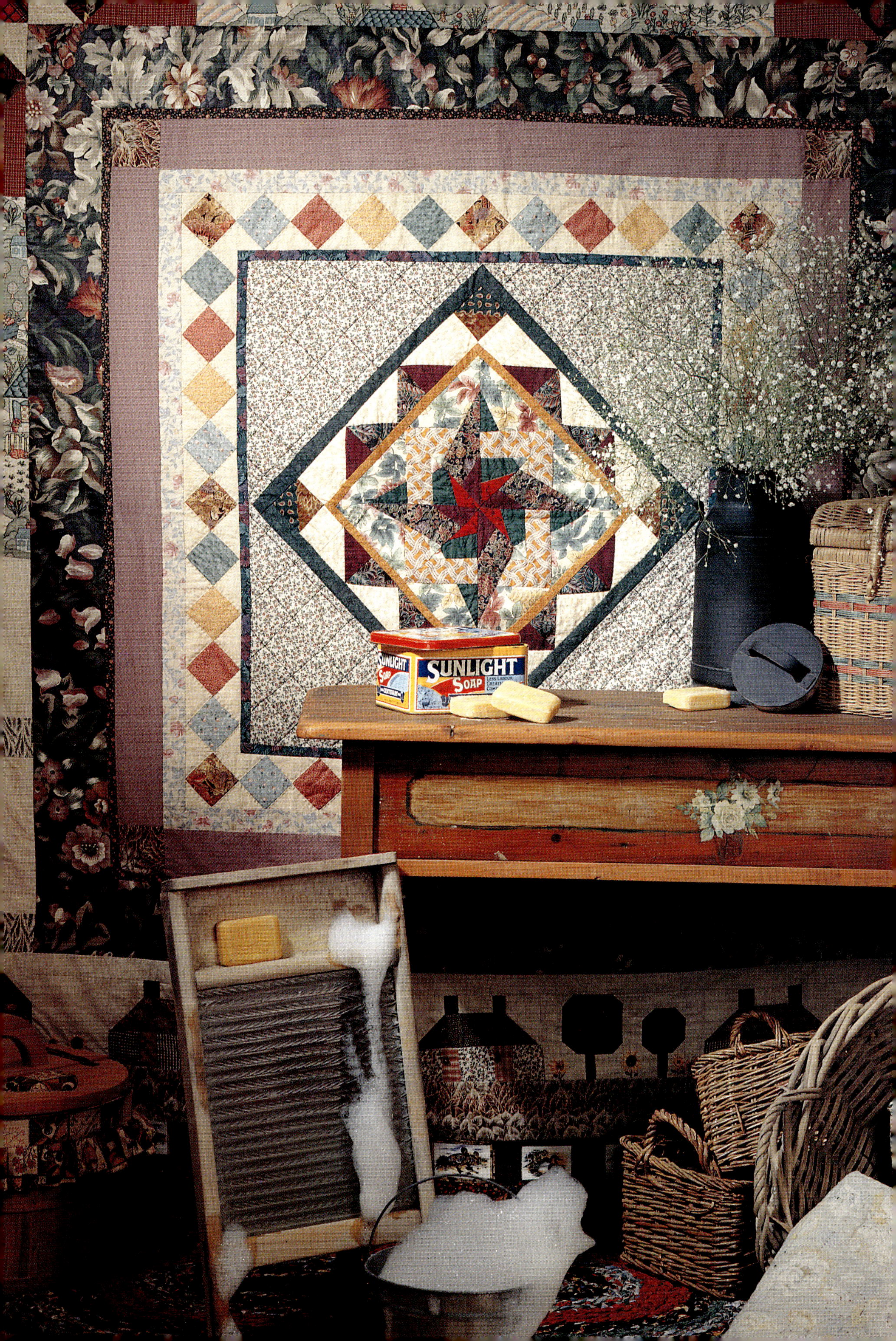
SUNLIGHT
SOAP

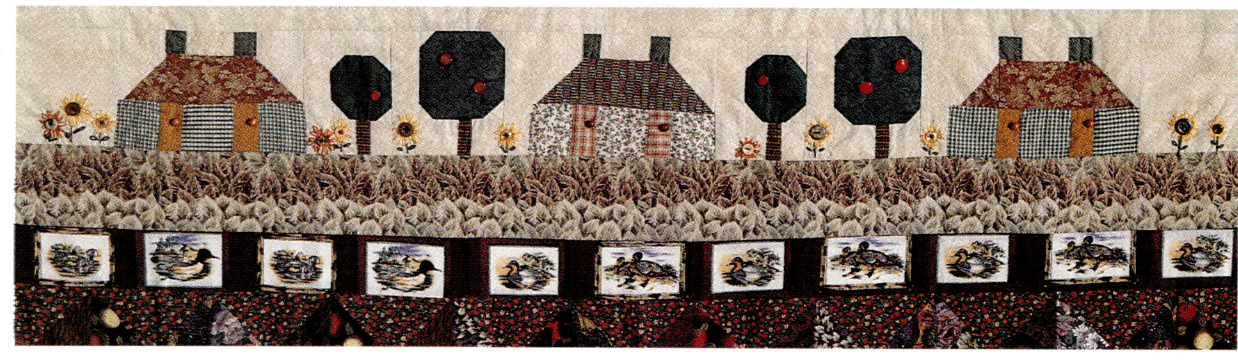

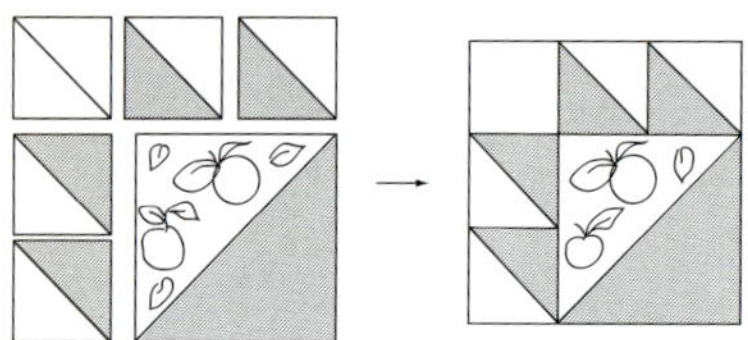

Diagram 4

7in x 7in, small cut 4in x 4in. Each block needs one background corner cut 3½in x 3½in. Make eight blocks.

Assemble your scenery, cottages, trees and baskets following the photographs.

ROUND SIX

Rebecca's quilt uses pictorial border prints for the last frame, and a 2in cut (1½in finished) dark float. Rebecca added a border of hearts (templates from Lizzie's Quilt) and triangles to match Round One to complete her quilt.

FINISHED SIZE

76in x 78in (193cm x 198cm)

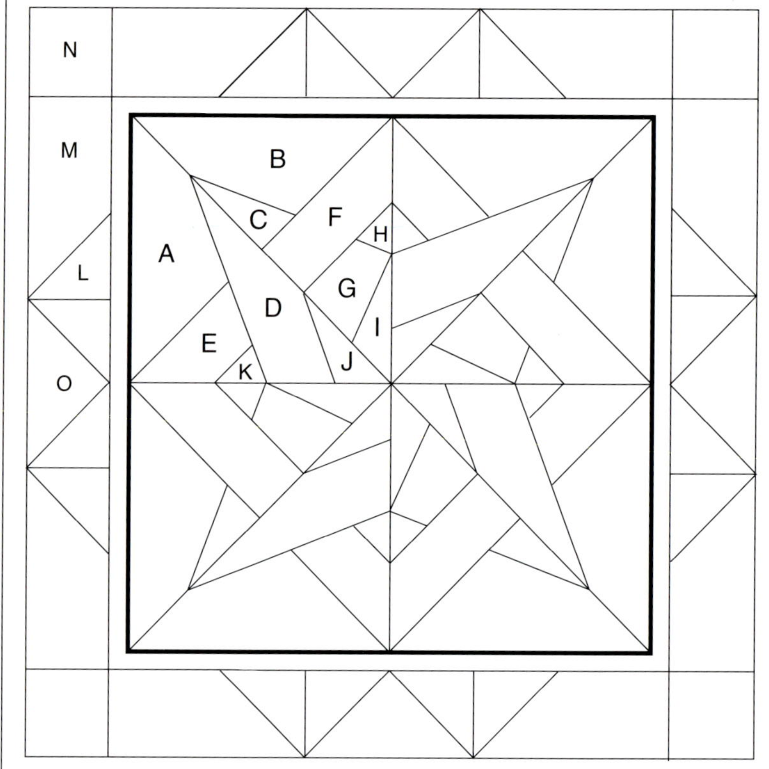

Block Diagram and Round One

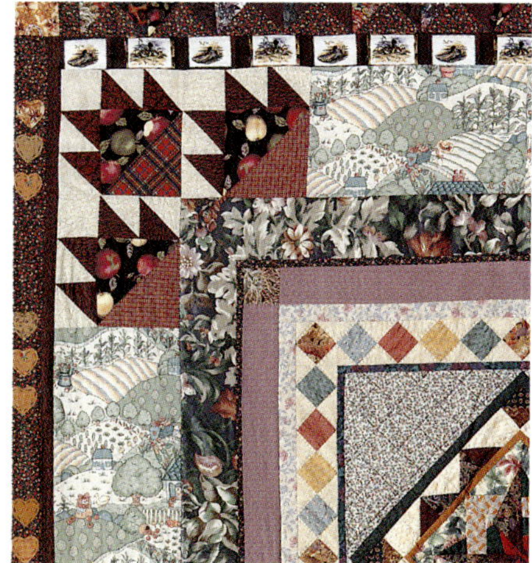

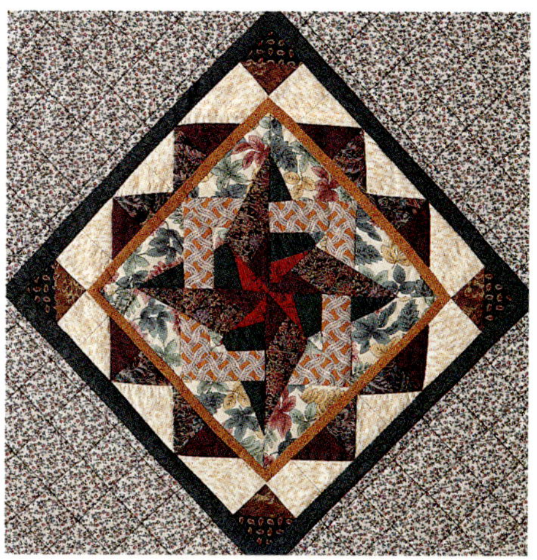

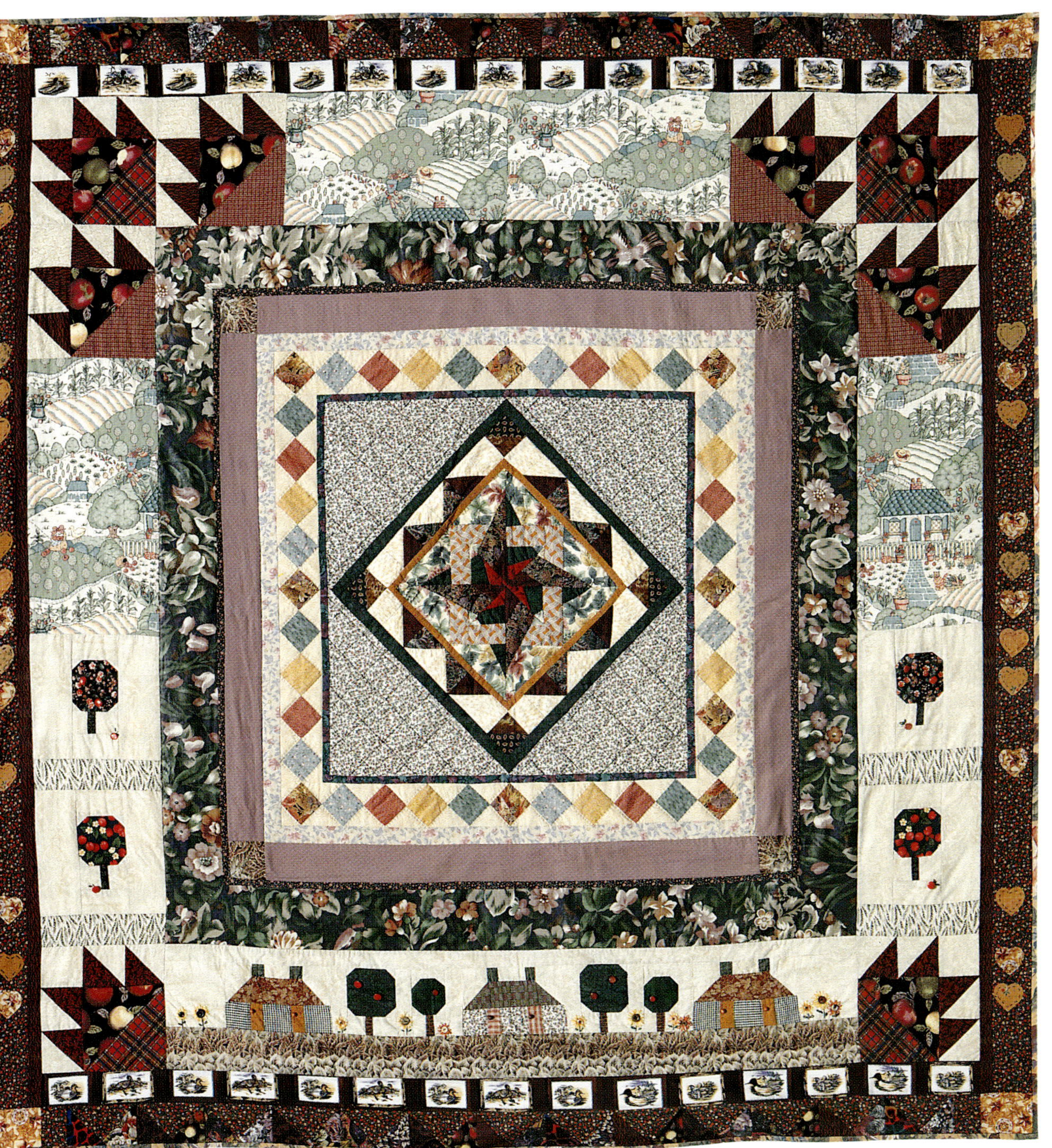

Rebecca Pring

Being the eldest daughter of Yan it was bound to happen! A quilter for four years, she has her own private stash – expanding this considerably after a trip to the USA. Rebecca makes bears and is often employed by the group when projects need to be framed.

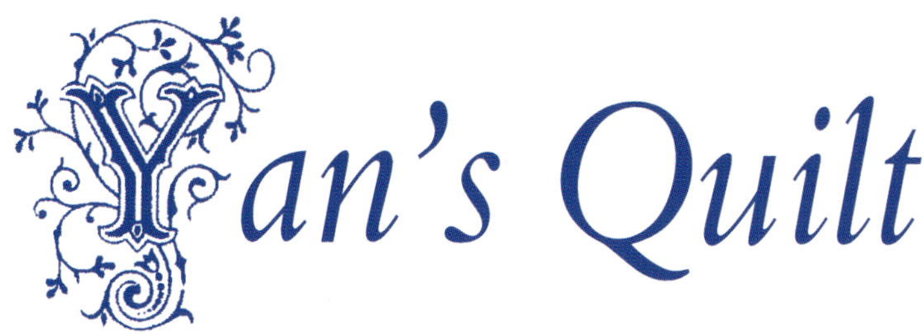

Yan's Quilt

The block at the beginning flashes with a rainbow of cottage garden colours set in a complex geometric medallion. A love of blue tones with yellow and cream is evident and sets the theme for the following rounds. Ruby reds and opal blues add fabulous highlights in soft backgrounds.

Read the Getting Started and Basic Instructions sections before you begin your quilt.

THE BLOCK

Cut and piece carefully using the block templates and the BLOCK DIAGRAM as a guide. Your block should measure 12in x 12in finished when complete.

ROUND ONE

Use templates to cut and piece fabrics. Yan's Quilt used 16 red and 16 blue triangles with cream background. The four corners use a dark multi-coloured floral.

ROUND TWO

Cut four large triangles (see diagram 1). You may wish to stabilise the bias edges with a row of stitching to prevent stretching. Attach the triangles by the long edge to the four sides of round one. Cut float strip in red 1½in wide (1in finished) and add to all four sides.

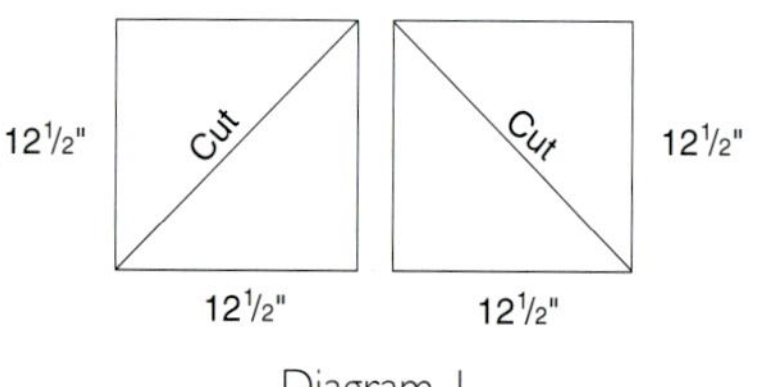

Diagram 1

ROUND THREE

Nine-patch blocks in medium florals float evenly in a soft blue background. See diagram 2 for block construction.

Nine patch block (make eight)

For each block cut five squares 2in x 2in in floral and four squares 2in x 2in in background fabric.

Connecting strips between the nine-patch blocks are cut 5in wide in the same background fabric as the blocks. Set the blocks and the connections as in photographs.

Cut float strip 1¼in wide (½in finished) and sew to four sides of the quilt to complete the round.

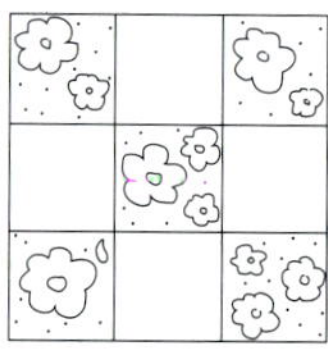

Diagram 2

ROUND FOUR

Bright jewel coloured bow ties sit one behind the other between midnight blue corners.

Use diagram 1 of Debbie's Quilt for construction of bow ties with new cutting sizes:

A. Cut two squares 2¼in x 2¼in (bow tie fabric)

B. Cut two squares 2¼in x 2¼in (background fabric)

C. Cut two squares 1¼in x 1¼in (bow tie fabric).

Make 40 bow ties.

Join bow ties with four corner squares cut 4in x 4in (see photographs for placement). Cut another opal blue float strip 1¼in wide (½in finished) and sew to the four sides of the quilt to complete the round.

ROUND FIVE

A dazzle of friendship stars spin in a wide float of antique cream.

Friendship Star Block (make 24)

For the four star points use instructions in diagram 1 Narelle's Quilt for half square triangles with squares cut 3in x 3in (this gives 2½in x 2½in squares for the star block). Cut four background squares 2½in x 2½in and one centre square 2½in x 2½in in star fabric. (Block measures 6in x 6in finished). See diagram 3.

Set the star blocks in groups of three with connecting strips of background fabric (cut 6½in wide) between. The connecting strips on Yan's Quilt measure 6½in x 8½in (6in x 7½in finished). Cut two for each side. Assemble stars and connecting strips.

Before attaching these to your quilt, cut float strip in background fabric 1½in wide (1in finished) and

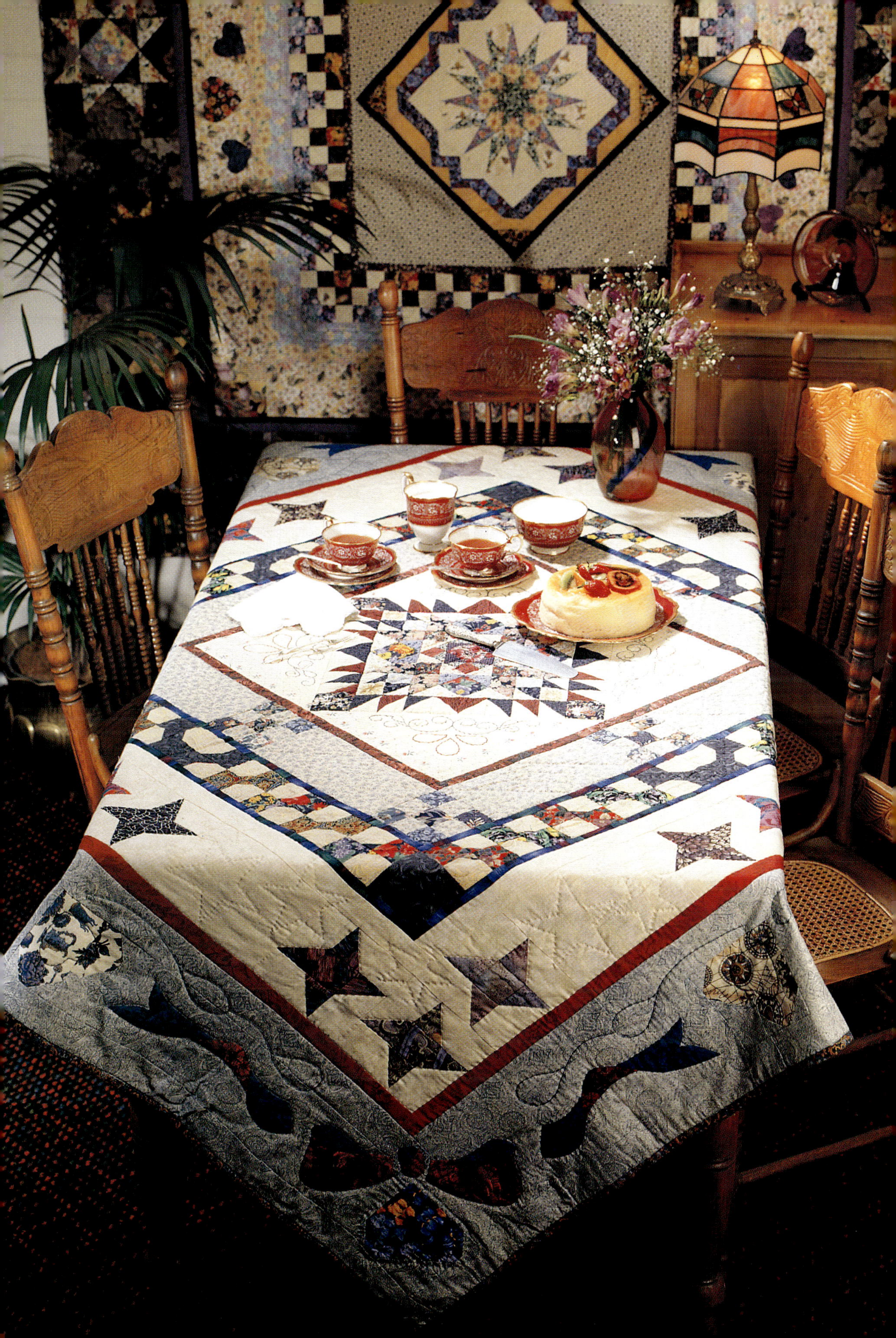

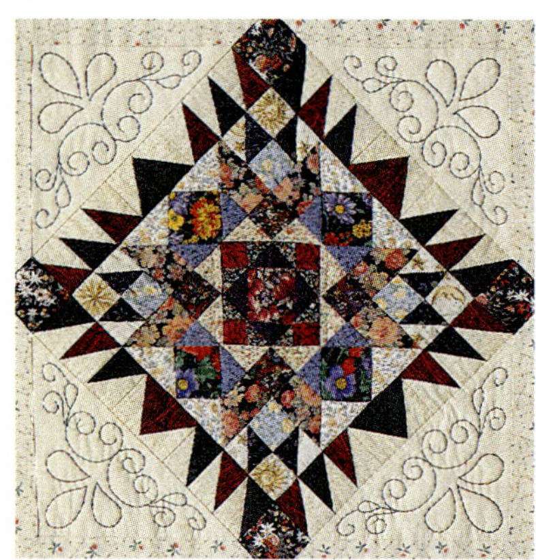

sew onto the last edge of Round Four. Join the star border sections to your quilt. Cut float strips in accent fabric $1^1/_2$in wide to sew onto the outer edge of this round (see photograph).

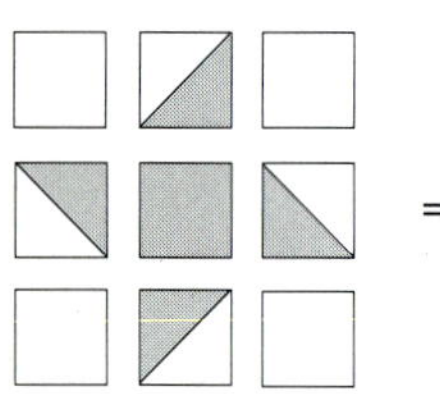
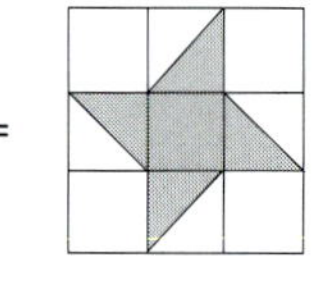

Diagram 3

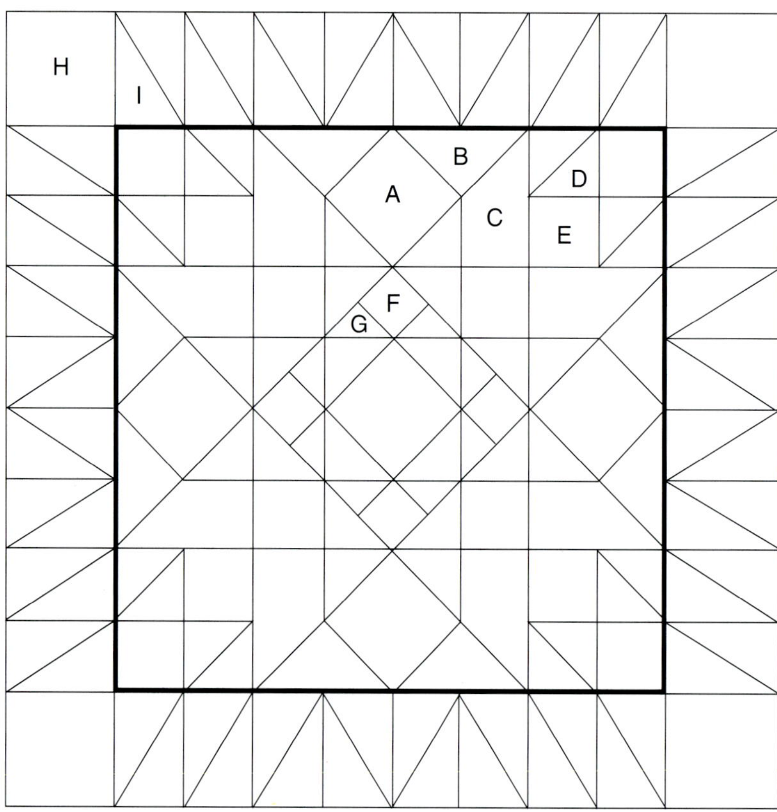

Block Diagram and Round One

ROUNDS SIX AND SEVEN

A border of large quick-pieced hearts with room for bows and tails in rich accent colours makes a charming finish to this quilt. Make hearts in soft florals with a pale background fabric.

First cut a float strip $2^1/_2$in wide (2in finished) of background fabric and sew onto the quilt. Make your large hearts following diagram 4.

Heart block (make 20)

For each heart cut:

One $3^1/_2$in x $5^1/_2$in (heart fabric)
One $3^1/_2$in x $2^1/_2$in (heart fabric)
One $2^1/_2$in x $2^1/_2$in (background fabric)
Four $1^3/_4$in x $1^3/_4$in (background fabric).

Set hearts in groups of four with spacer strips between (cut 2in wide). Cut a connecting strip $5^1/_2$in wide (5in finished) to join centre groups to outer corners. Follow photographs to complete your assembly, finally adding another float strip to the outside edge cut $2^1/_2$in wide (2in finished).

Bows and Tails templates are included on the pull-out pattern sheet for you to appliqué - remember to add seam allowance to suit your favourite appliqué technique.

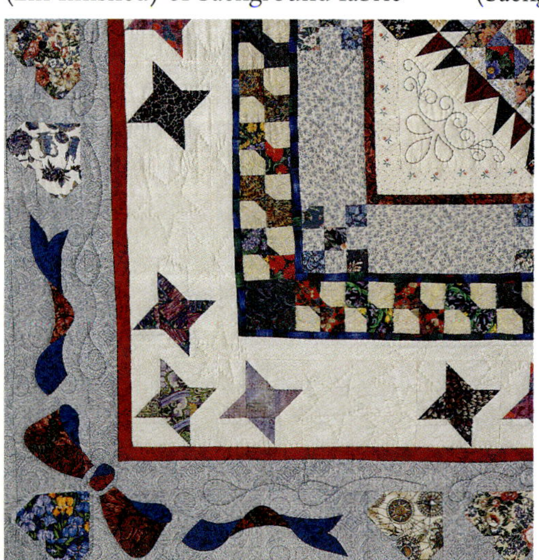

FINISHED SIZE

78in x 78in (198cm x 198cm)

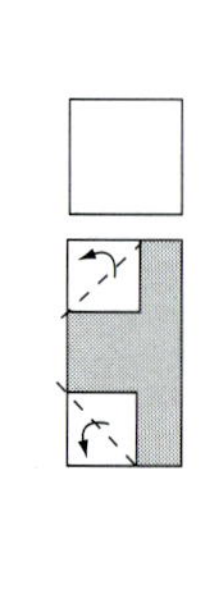
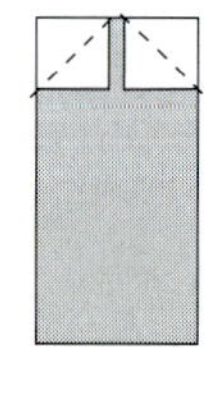
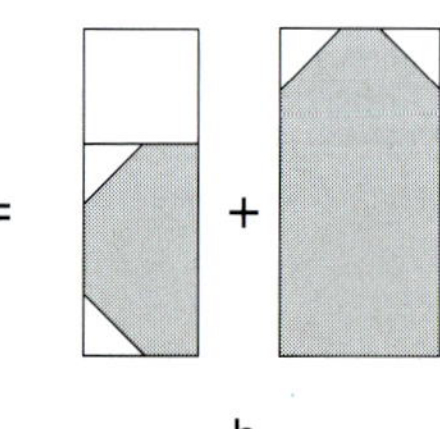
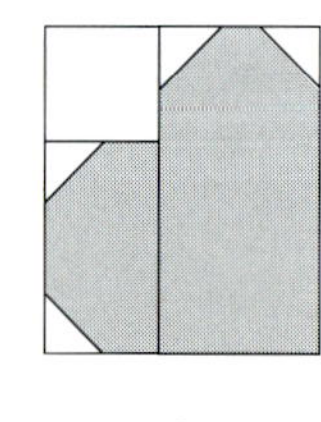

Diagram 4

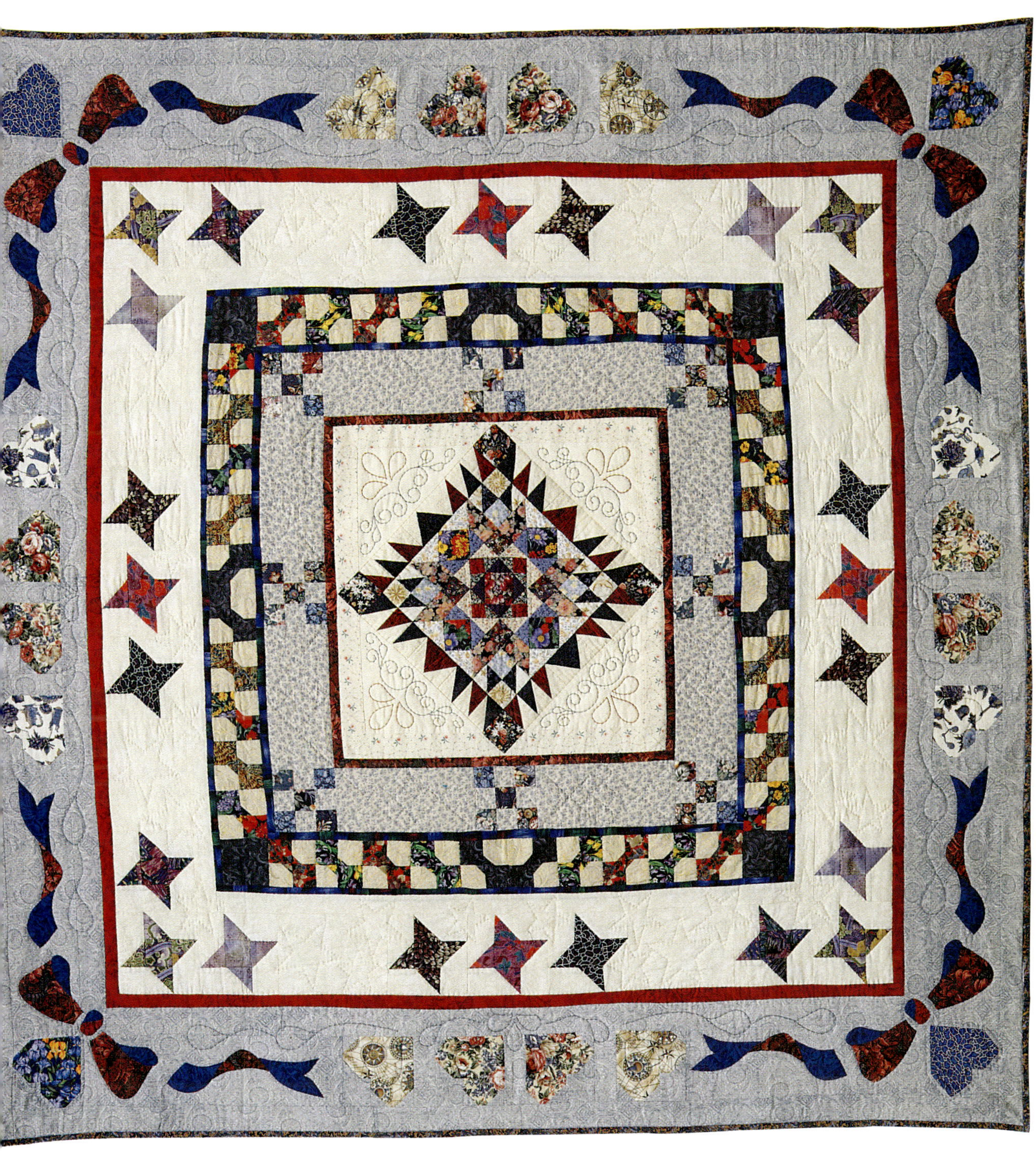

Yan Pring

Yan is a quilt tutor who began quilting as soon as a class started 15 years ago and now it has become an important part of the week. 'Colourwash' has provided the perfect excuse to keep buying beautiful fabric. She lives up to the family description "Our mum doesn't cook, she quilts".

Basic Equipment

We may have come a long way since quilts were first made in the 1800s, but the basic tools for patchwork are still the same. Needles, thread, pins and scissors remain the essentials.

NEEDLES

If machine stitching your quilt a supply of new sewing machine needles for light to medium-weight cottons is required.

For both hand piecing and quilting, a 'between' needle is considered the best. When a longer needle is required, 'sharps' are used. A good general rule is to use as fine a needle as you can manage comfortably; size 8 is recommended for beginners. As you progress you may want to switch to a smaller needle in order to make smaller stitches; size 12 is the smallest needle.

THREAD

Traditional advice is for synthetic threads to be used with synthetic fabrics and cotton with cotton fabrics. 100 per cent cotton thread or polyester-cotton thread (which is a polyester core wrapped in cotton) are the best for cotton fabrics; they are also the easiest to use for all other fabrics. Sometimes the polyester-cotton thread has a tendency to fray and tangle. This can be avoided by knotting the end before unrolling the thread, then cutting and threading the other end through the needle.

Select a colour that matches the darkest fabric you are sewing. If you are using a lot of different fabrics, select a neutral thread that will blend inconspicuously with all of them, such as grey or ecru.

PINS

Glass-headed pins are very sharp and good for piercing straight through the material when lining up a seam or starting point.

A longer pin is available, and this is excellent for pinning together layers on more bulky projects.

SCISSORS

You will need three pairs of scissors for patchwork. Dressmaker's shears, preferably with a bent handle, should be extremely sharp; use them only for cutting fabric. You will also need a pair of scissors for cutting paper; never cut paper with your sewing shears, as this will dull your blades. Embroidery scissors are used for clipping threads and seam allowances; these should also be very sharp.

ROTARY CUTTER AND MAT

Once you have used a rotary cutter, you will wonder how you ever lived without it. It is an excellent tool for cutting strips, straightening fabric edges and even cutting out a variety of geometric patchwork pieces. It also makes possible more accurate cutting of several layers of fabric at one time. Choose a cutter with a large blade, and keep spare blades handy. Always cut on a mat specially designed for a rotary cutter to keep the blade sharp; the mat will grip the fabric and help the blade to cut straight. A 'self-healing' cutting mat is ideal.

RULERS

A long clear plastic ruler is an absolute must to use with a rotary cutter. They are well marked and sturdy, so there is no danger of shaving off a piece of the ruler when cutting layers of fabric.

PENCILS

A soft lead pencil is the traditional option for marking a design, but there is also a variety of marking pencils available. One of these is a water-soluble pencil and this is probably the most useful, as it fades after a period of time. However, you do have to be careful with this, as the design is liable to disappear before the project can be finished.

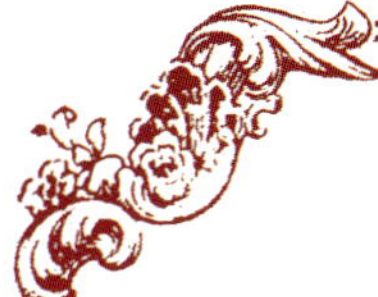
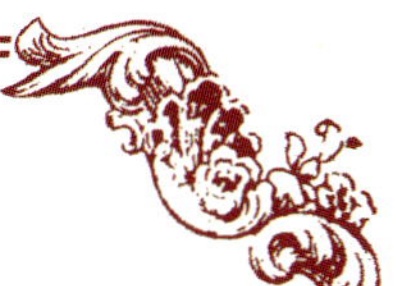

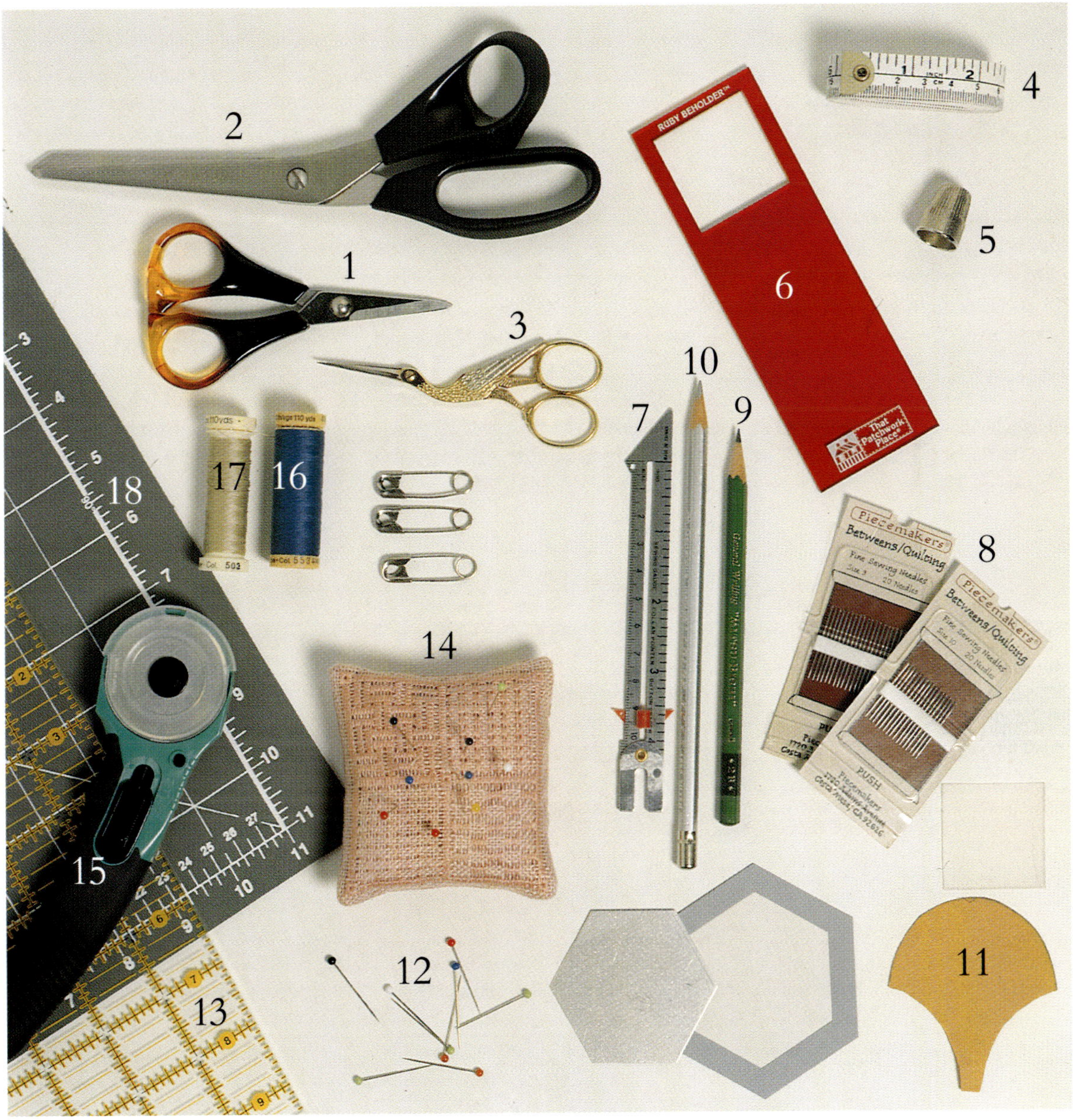

1 Paper Cutting Scissors

2 Dressmakers' Scissors

3 Embroidery Scissors

4 Tape Measure

5 Thimble

6 Ruby Beholder

7 Adjustable Ruler

8 Needles

9 HB Pencil

10 Silver Marking Pencil

11 Templates

12 Glass Headed Pins

13 Plastic Ruler

14 Pin Cushion

15 Rotary Cutter

16 100% Cotton Thread

17 Cotton/Polyester thread

18 Cutting Mat

TEMPLATES

Templates can be homemade from graph paper or tracing paper and cardboard. However, the edges of cardboard templates tend to wear after frequent cutting of patches. Plastic and metal templates are available in a great variety of shapes and sizes and are virtually indestructible - a great advantage, especially for a large project which requires cutting out several of each shape.

Window templates are particularly useful if you are featuring or centring a motif or flower in a patch.

THIMBLES

A thimble is absolutely indispensable if you are quilting by hand. A thimble is also a good idea for the finger underneath the work to push the needle back through the fabric.

FRAMES AND HOOPS

A frame or a hoop makes the quilting of large projects, such as bed-sized quilts, a lot easier. Although it is not absolutely necessary for smaller items, a better finish is obtained if one is used.

FABRICS

Choosing the most suitable fabric for your patchwork project is important, especially for a beginner. There is no doubt that some fabrics are much easier to work with than others and experience will teach you which fabric is a joy to use and which is an absolute headache. However, the most important rules to remember are always buy the best fabric you can afford and, to begin with at least, use a firmly woven, lightweight, 100 per cent pure cotton because it is easier to use, lasts longer and gives crisp results.

Synthetics and mixtures can be difficult to iron and handle and occasionally may pucker along the seams. Nevertheless they are attractive, versatile and can be unusual or striking in appearance. They are often more readily available than 100 per cent cottons, though some tend to be slippery, floppy and soft.

As you become more experienced you may well want to experiment with other more exotic fabrics. Many of these will need special handling but the only way to learn about these fabrics is to test them for yourself. Some satins and taffeta may prove to be too fragile for patchwork. Synthetics also tend to be more difficult to quilt.

CHOICE OF COLOUR AND PRINTS

The successful combining of colours is often a matter of trial and error and not something that can be taught. The only way you are going to discover if it is going to work is by trying it.

Value or the lightness or darkness of a colour is probably more important than actual colour when you are making a quilt. To achieve successful results you should try and use a range of values.

Many small-scale floral prints are available. Although a safe choice, they can sometimes be so safe and so well colour-coordinated that they result in a rather dull and uninspired finished effect. Experiment with prints of varying scale, stripes and border designs, geometric prints and checks. Some large-scale prints can introduce a delicate, lacy effect. Particular care must be taken with stripes because, if they are not cut and sewn perfectly straight, it will be very obvious.

It is also worth noting that certain fabrics are evocative of different eras or styles. You can create a country-style quilt by including fabrics which are bold and brightly coloured. A 1930s-style quilt can be created by including fabrics such as bright pastels, fresh florals, perky checks, stripes and white backgrounds.

FABRICS TO AVOID

Stretch fabrics such as knits and some crêpes should be avoided. Very closely woven fabrics can also prove too difficult even for machine sewing. This applies to heavy fabrics such as canvas, and lightweight fabrics like some poplins. Very open weave fabrics can cause difficulties with fraying and transparency.

PREPARATION OF FABRICS

Always wash your fabrics before use. This will pre-shrink them, remove excess dye and remove any sizing, making the fabric easier to handle. Machine washing is good, unless you have a very small quantity of fabric.

The volume of water used seems to flush the dye and sizing out thoroughly. Problems are unusual, but if you are suspicious of a fabric it would be wise to handwash it separately. If using the tumble dryer, a very short time is sufficient, unless the pieces are very large. Be careful not to over-dry the fabrics, as they may become very creased.

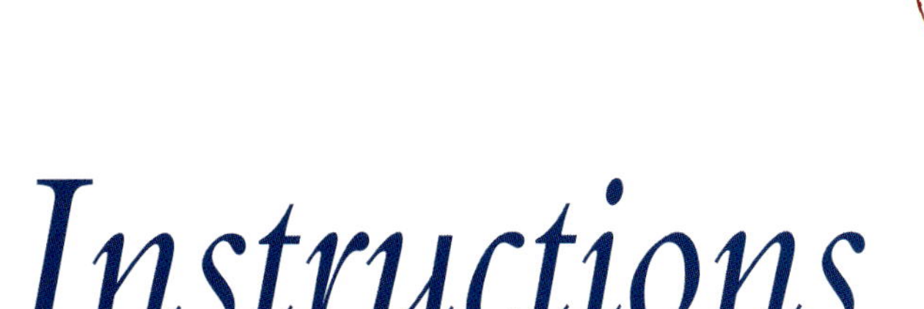

Basic Instructions

Patchwork quilts can be made in any number of ways. Here you will find the basic techniques that are required to successfully complete a quilt.

DESIGN AND DRAFTING

When you want to adapt a design or border, or simply see how the quilt will look and fit together, you will need to make a sketch on graph paper.

Graph paper is used for two reasons; first, to make small sketches of quilt designs (graph plan) and second, to make full size drawings of shapes for templates or as guides for rotary cutting.

A graph plan allows you to play with different colourings and is a map to which you can refer as you construct your quilt. It will help you see the relative proportions of the border and quilt in order to judge the effect. Best of all, your sketch lets you preview your quilt and make improvements before you start cutting and sewing.

Your quilt sketch is a drawing of your quilt in miniature and you will need to assign a scale in order to calculate the finished size of your quilt and to draft templates. Keep the scale easy to ensure cutting dimensions that will match standard markings on your rotary cutting ruler.

DRAFTING TEMPLATES

Quarter inch graph paper is one of the easiest to use to make full size drawings of shapes for templates. You can draw a full

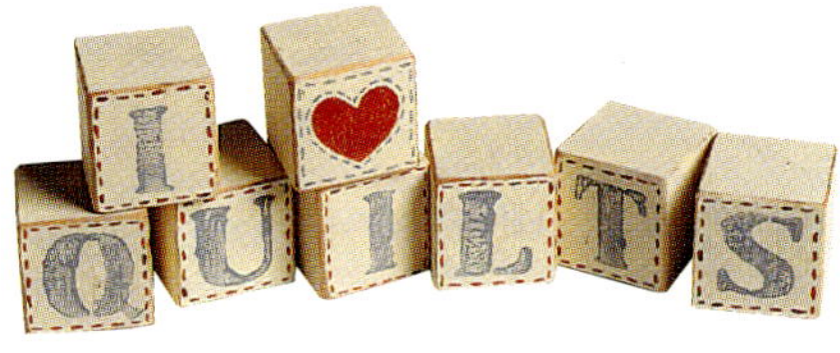

size block or portion of a border on to graph paper and identify each shape that needs to be cut by lightly colouring it in, and add a consistent ¼in seam allowance around each shape. Trace the completed shapes onto template material or use the measurements as cutting guides for template-free rotary cutting.

Template plastic with a ¼in grid is also available, so that shapes can be drawn directly on to it and an accurate seam allowance added. If the templates are going to be used for machine sewing a ¼in seam allowance will need to be added all round. If the template is being used for hand sewing a ¼in seam allowance can be added when cutting out the fabric. Straight grain arrows should be marked onto templates.

NOTE: The outside edges of a block or quilt must always be on the straight grain, otherwise your quilt will not lie flat. Mark your graphed blocks and borders accordingly.

Gluing a piece of sandpaper to the back of a paper or plastic template, with the gritty side facing down, is a great way of cutting accurate shapes from fabric. The sandpaper adds weight and sturdiness to the template, and the rough surface grips the fabric for more accurate cutting.

NOTE: DO NOT CUT SANDPAPER WITH YOUR FABRIC SCISSORS.

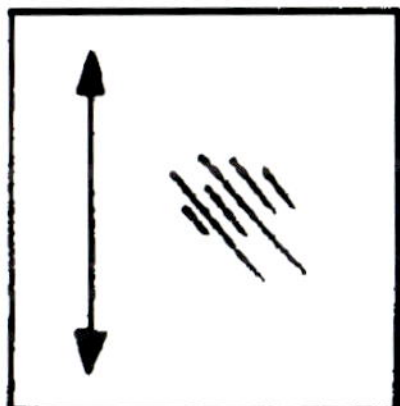

Standard Template

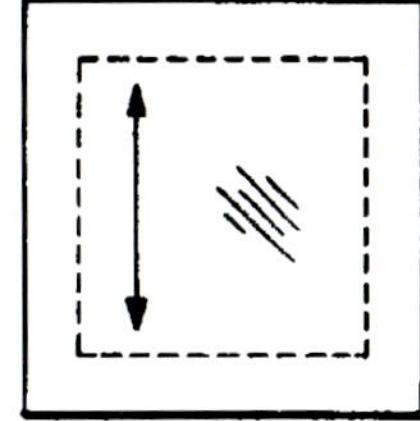

Machine Sewing template

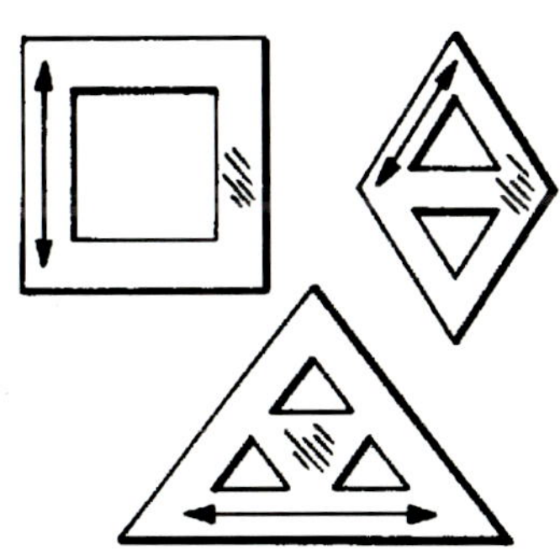

Window Template

CUTTING

Trim the selvedge from your fabric before you begin cutting. If you are using one fabric for both borders and block pieces, cut the borders first and then the block pieces from what is left over.

Position the templates on your fabric so the arrows match the straight grain of the fabric. With a sharp pencil (either an erasable pencil or a white for dark fabrics or lead pencil for light fabrics), trace around the template on the fabric. Remember to allow a further $^{1}/_{4}$in all around the drawn shape for seam allowance before cutting out. Templates for machine sewing usually include a seam allowance but these pieces must be precisely cut as there is no drawn line to guide your sewing.

Multiple layers can be cut at the one time by folding and pressing your fabric into layers before laying the template on.
Remember to make sure that each piece is cut on the straight grain.

ROTARY (OR TEMPLATE FREE) CUTTING

It is important to use your rotary cutter accurately and efficiently to ensure straight pieces. The first step is to straighten the fabric by folding the fabric in layers, selvedge to selvedge to fit on your

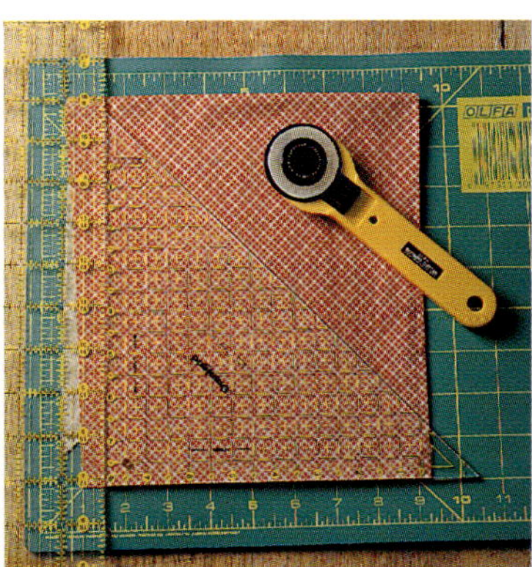

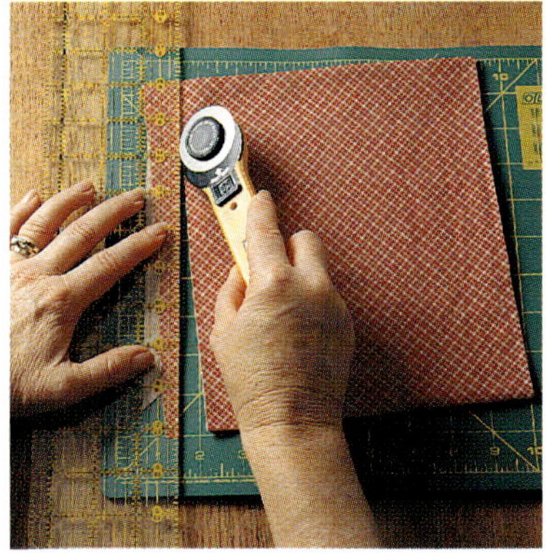

cutting mat. Lay a triangle along the folded edge of the fabric and push it against the right side of the ruler until it is just at the edge.

Hold the ruler down with your left hand, remove the triangle and begin cutting. Walk your hand up parallel with the cutter and continue to cut off the end of the fabric. Do not try to hold the ruler at the bottom as you will more than likely move it.

Once you have straightened your fabric you can use your cutter and ruler to cut strips of fabric to whatever width you require.

Squares, rectangles and triangles are all cut from strips. Remember when cutting squares and rectangles to add $^{1}/_{2}$in to the desired finished measurement, for example a 2in finished square needs to be cut $2^{1}/_{2}$in square. For a 2in x 4in finished rectangle, cut $2^{1}/_{2}$in x $4^{1}/_{2}$in.

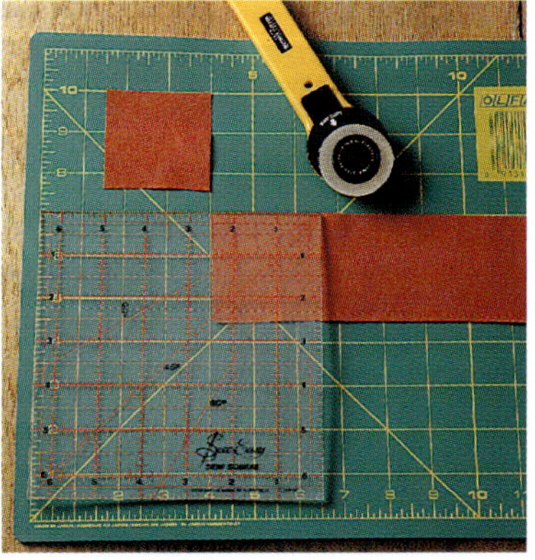

Half square triangles are half a square with the short sides on the straight grain and the long side on the bias. To cut these triangles, cut a square in half diagonally. Cut the square $^{7}/_{8}$in larger than the finished short side of the triangle to allow for all seam allowances.

Quarter square triangles are used along the outside edge of a quilt and some blocks are quarter square triangles. These triangles have their short sides on the bias and the long side on the straight grain. These triangles are cut from squares. Each square is cut into four on the diagonal. Each square is $1^{1}/_{4}$in larger than the finished long side of the triangle.

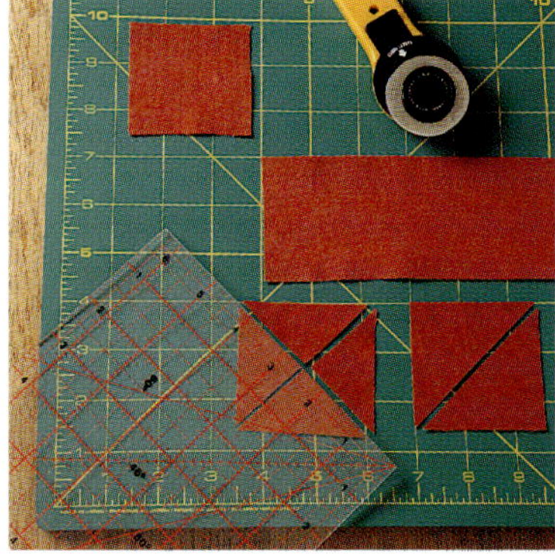

PIECING METHODS

HAND PIECING

Pieces for hand piecing require precisely marked seam lines; marked cutting lines are optional. To mark patches, place the template face down on the wrong side of the fabric and draw around it accurately with a sharp pencil. Leave space between patches for a $^{1}/_{4}$in seam allowance when cutting.

After marking the patches, cut outward from the seam line $^{1}/_{4}$in, measuring the distance by eye. The pieces will be joined right sides together, so the marked seam line on the wrong side of the fabric will be visible on both sides of the patchwork when sewing. Sew the seam through the pencilled lines with a short running stitch and occasional back stitch, using a single thread. Begin and end each seam at the seam line (not at the edge of fabric) with two or three back stitches to secure the seam and only sew from point to point and not edge to edge.

When joining blocks and rows together do not sew the seam allowance down. Instead, sew right up to the dot marking the corner and then begin on the next side by again taking a couple of small back stitches and continue sewing. By doing this, you leave your options open as to which way you press the seam allowance then the block is completed.

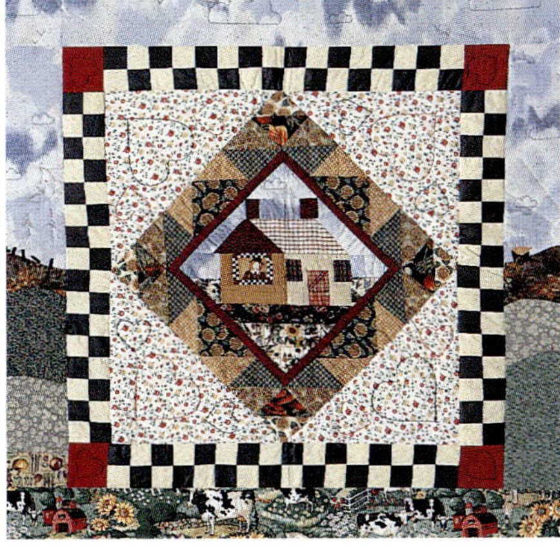

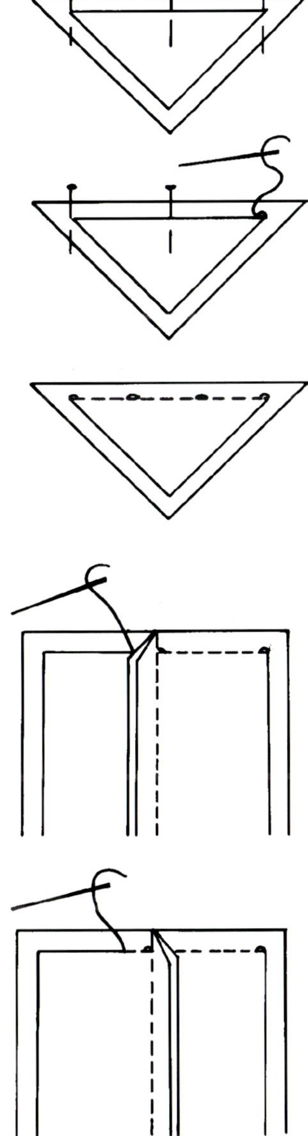

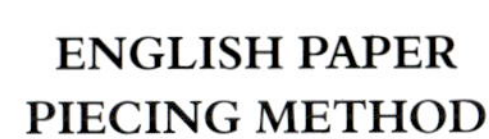

ENGLISH PAPER PIECING METHOD

This handpiecing technique involves basting fabric over a thin cardboard or paper template. The shapes are then stitched together to form blocks and ultimately to form a quilt. Although this method is time-consuming, it results in precise, sharp seams and a very professional finished appearance. It also has the advantage of being able to be picked up, put down and carried around.

When handpiecing over paper it is necessary to cut out an exact sized light cardboard template for every piece of the pattern, as well as a cardboard pattern for every piece. Cut out the fabric shape using your cardboard pattern and remember to include a ¼in seam allowance all around the shape.

Place the cardboard template in the centre of the wrong side of the fabric shape. Working one side at a time, fold over the seam allowance onto the template and tack into place through the template (make sure the corners of the fabric are neatly folded in). For easy removal of the tacking it is a good idea to start with a knot and to finish with a simple double stitch.

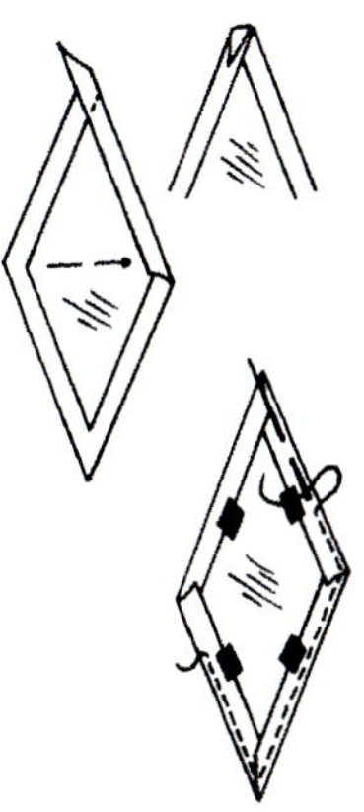

To join the patches together, place them right sides together and match corners. With a matching thread, or a mid-grey thread which blends with most colours, join the edges from corner to corner using a tiny whip stitch and double stitch the corners. The stitch should be fairly small and not visible from the right side of the fabric. Make each block separately by sewing

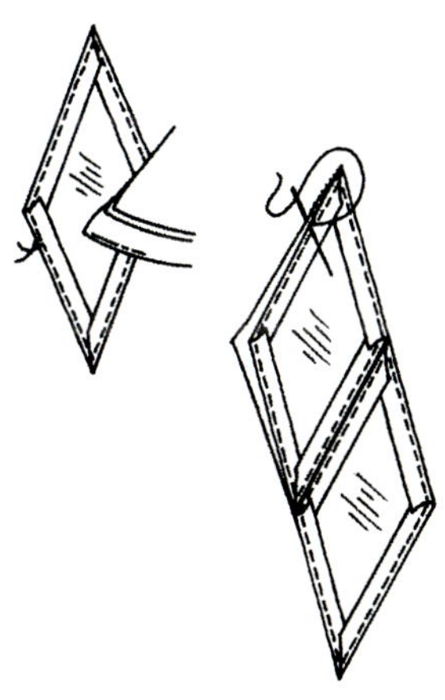

the smallest pieces together first to form units. Join smaller units to form larger ones until the block is complete. Press after making, then join the blocks together to form rows and the rows together to form the sampler or quilt top.

The cardboard templates can be removed when all the pieces are joined together. Turn the quilt over, press well with a warm iron, allow to cool before carefully removing the tacking stitches and lifting out each piece of cardboard separately.

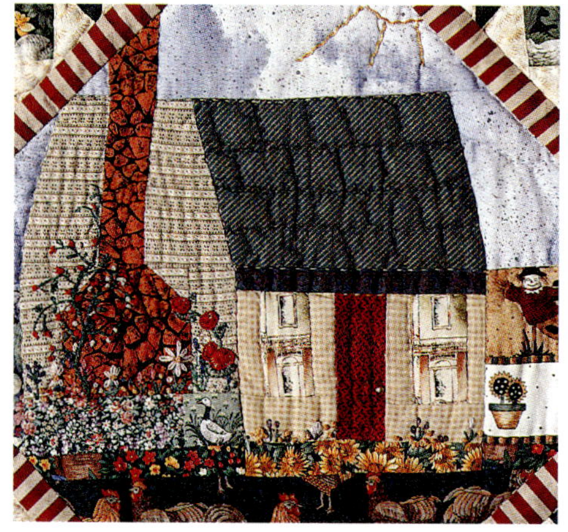

MACHINE PIECING

Accurate cutting is very important in machine piecing. Include seam allowances in the template and mark the cutting line on the back of the fabric.

Use white or neutral thread as light in colour as the lightest colour in the project. Use a dark neutral thread for piecing dark solids.

When machine sewing patches, align cut edges with the edge of the presser foot if it is 1/4in wide. If not, place masking tape on the throat plate of the machine 1/4in away from the needle to guide you in making 1/4in seams. Sew all the way to the cut edge unless you are inserting a patch into an angle. Short seams need not be pinned unless matching is involved if the seam is long. Keep pins away from the seam line.

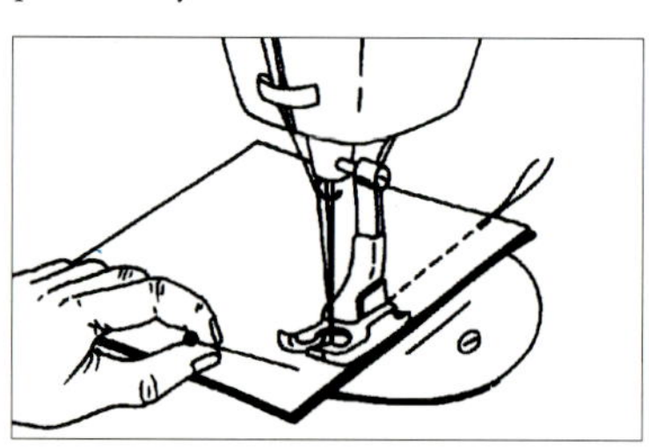

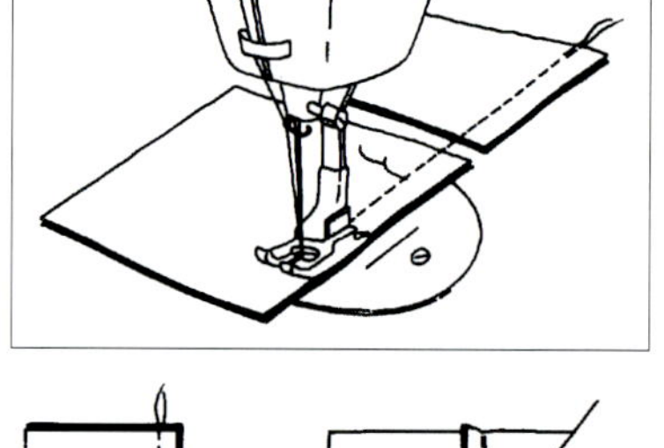

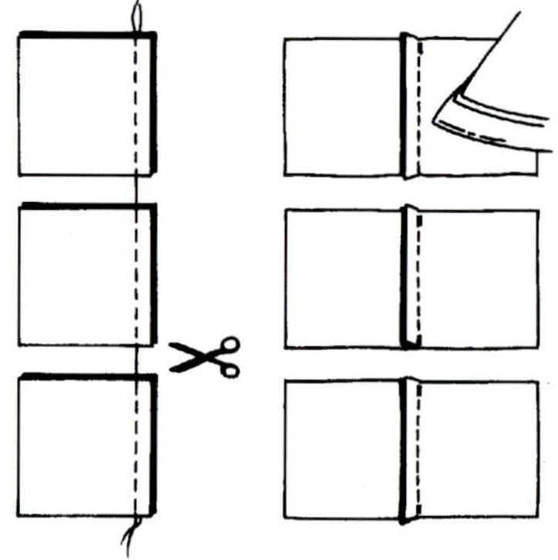

Sewing over pins is not good for your sewing machine needles.

Use chain piecing whenever possible to save time and thread. To chain piece, sew one seam, but do not lift the presser foot. Do not take the piece out of the sewing machine and do not cut the thread. Instead, set up the next piece to be sewn and continue stitching. There will be little twists of thread between the two pieces. Sew all the seams you can at one time in this way, then remove the 'chain'. Clip the threads. When joining rows, make sure matching seam allowances are pressed in opposite directions to reduce bulk and make matching easier. Pin pieces together directly through stitching and to the right or left of the seam, remove pins as you sew.

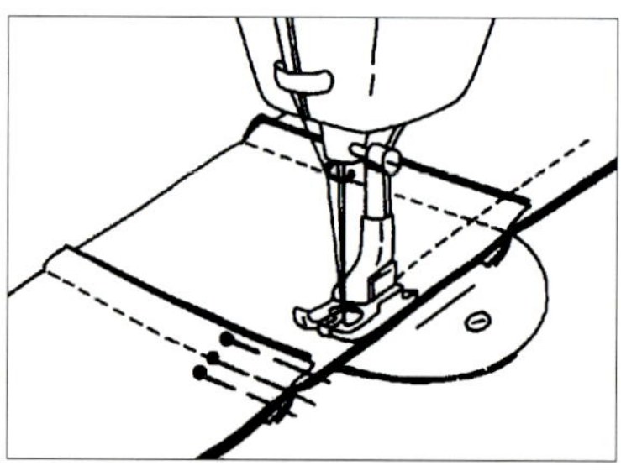

METHODS OF JOINING BLOCKS

BLOCKS JOINED EDGE-TO-EDGE

Join the blocks to form strips the width of the quilt. First pin each seam very carefully, inserting a pin wherever seams meet, at right angles to the seam. Stitch using a 1/4in seam allowance. Then join all blocks in the second row, and so on, until all rows are completed. Press all seam allowances in the odd-numbered rows in one direction and all seam allowances in even-numbered rows in the opposite direction. When all rows are completed, pin two rows together so that seam lines match perfectly. Join rows in groups of two, then four, and so on, until the top is completed. Press all allowances in one direction, either up or down.

BLOCKS JOINED WITH VERTICAL AND HORIZONTAL SASHINGS

Join the blocks into strips with a vertical sash between each pair of blocks. Sew a horizontal piece of sashing to each strip, then join the strips to form the quilt top.

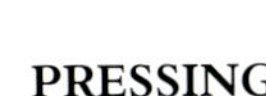

PRESSING

Press all seam allowances to one side, usually towards the darker fabric. Press quilt blocks flat and square with no puckers. To correct any problems in blocks, sashes or borders, remove a few stitches to ease puckers and re-sew.

APPLIQUE

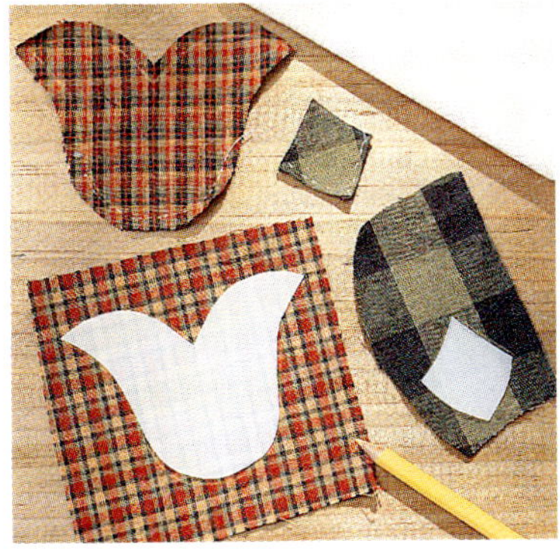

Appliqué is not a difficult technique but basic rules do apply. Curved shapes should be smooth with no points, points should be a definite point, and there should be no puckers. Begin by marking around the template onto the right side of the fabric. Cut out the shape with a ¼in or 6mm seam allowance. Turn the seam allowance under and baste. When there is a sharp curve sew a tiny running stitch just to the outside of the marked line. Gather this slightly and you will find the curve will sit well.

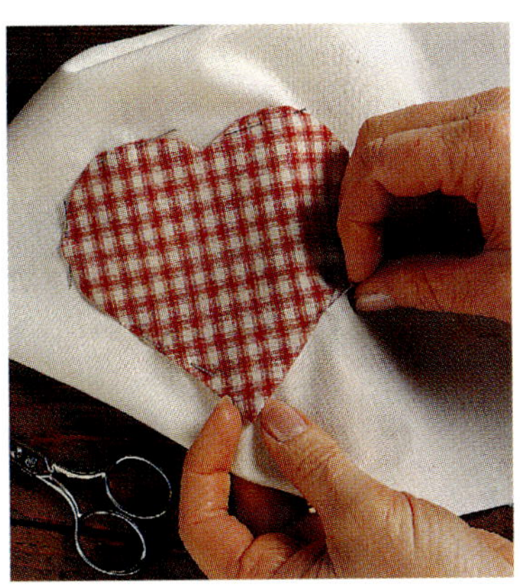

(see diagram 1). Where there is a sharp point, mitre the corner as you are basting and cut away any excess fabric. Be careful not to cut away too much. Pin the pieces to the background fabric making sure they are centred.

Cut a 40cm length of thread and make a small knot. Making sure the knot sits underneath the piece being appliquéd, bring the thread from the back through the background fabric and catch a couple of threads on the appliqué piece. Begin to appliqué making sure the needle enters the background fabric directly opposite where it came out on the top piece and slightly under the piece being appliquéd (see diagram 2). When you have completed stitching, finish off on the back with a couple of small back stitches.

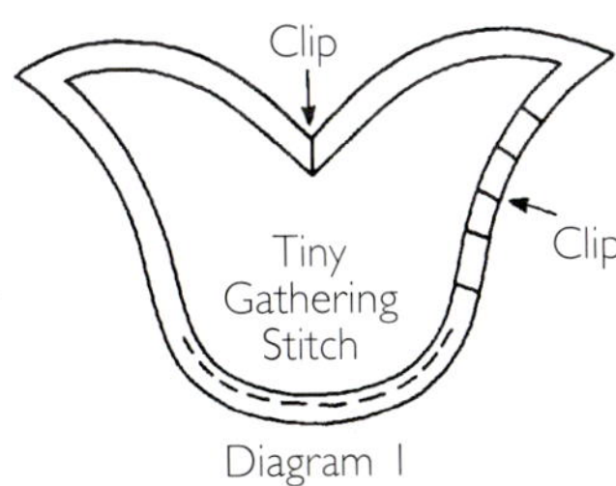

Diagram 1

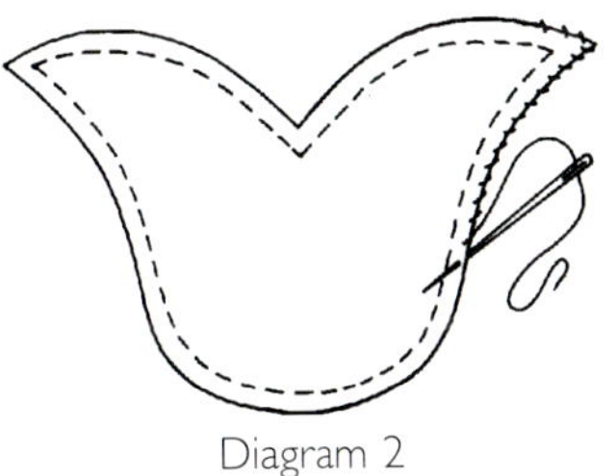

Diagram 2

ADDING MITRED BORDERS

Centre a border strip on each side of the quilt top to extend equally at each end. Pin, baste, and sew strips in ¼in seams, beginning and ending the stitching at the seam line, not at

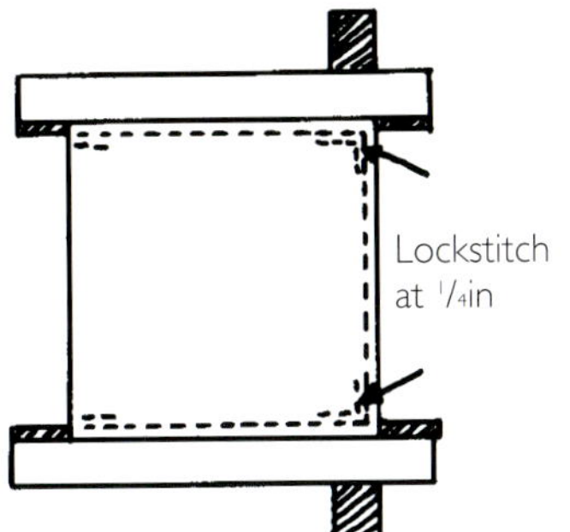

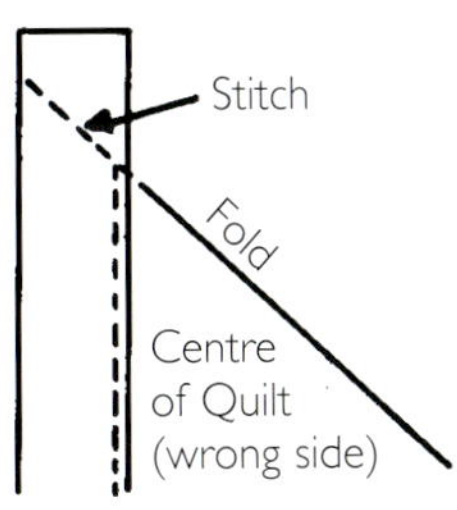

outer edge of the fabric. At one corner (on the wrong side), smooth one border over the adjacent one and draw a diagonal line from the inner seam line to the point where the outer edges of the two borders cross. Reverse the two borders (the bottom one is now on top), and again draw a diagonal line from the inner seam line to the point where the outer edges cross. Match the two pencil lines (fabrics right sides together), and sew through them. Cut away excess and press allowances open. Repeat at the other corners of the quilt.

BATTING

Batting is the padding that plumps up the quilt. It goes between the quilt top and the backing. There is a variety of battings on the market these days, ranging from natural fibres such as cotton and wool to synthetics. Most battings are available in different weights, but a thin, lightweight batting is ideal for hand quilting, making it

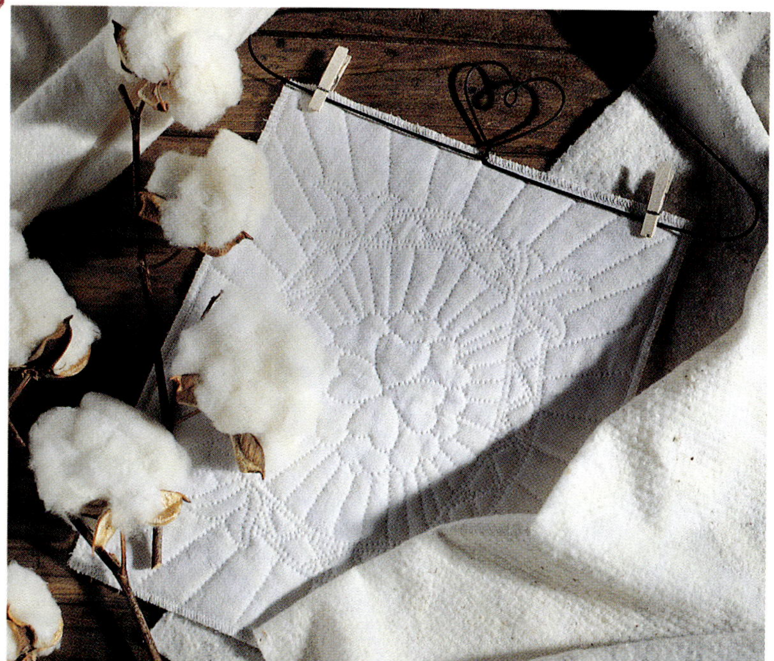

much easier to produce small, even stitches. A thin batting also gives a more authentic appearance to traditional quilt designs. However, the thicker battings are useful if you want extra warmth and they can be tied rather than quilted.

LINING

Make quilt lining about 2in larger on each side than the quilt top. Usually the two or three lengths that need to be sewn must be seamed together. Remove selvedges to avoid puckers; press seam allowances open or to one side. Place lining, wrong side up, on a flat surface. Spread quilt batting over the lining, making sure that both stay smooth and even. Place the quilt top, right side up, on top of the batting. Pin layers as necessary to secure them while basting. Beginning in the centre, baste in an 'X'. Working outwards, baste rows 4in and 6in apart. Finally, baste all around the edges.

MARKING FOR QUILTING

Place a quilting pattern under the quilt top. Lightly mark the design on the quilt top, using a hard lead pencil. Mark dark-coloured fabrics with a chalk pencil. Be sure to test water-soluble pens for removability before marking the quilt. Some quilting may be done without marking the top. Outline quilting (1/4in from seam around patches) or quilting in the ditch (right next to the seam on the side without the seam allowances) can be done by 'marking' the cutting line by eye. Other straight lines may also be marked as you quilt by using a piece of masking tape that is pulled away after a line is quilted along its edge.

QUILTING

Quilting is done in a short running stitch with a single strand of thread that goes through all three layers. Use a short needle (8 or 9 betweens) with about 18in or 45cm of thread. Make a small knot in the thread and take a first long stitch (about 1in or 2.5cm) through the top and batting only, coming up where the quilting will begin. Tug on the thread to pull the knotted end between the layers. Take straight, even stitches that are the same size on the top and bottom of the quilt. For tiny stitches, push the needle with a thimble on your middle finger; guide the fabric in front of the needle with the thumb of your hand above the quilt and with the thumb and index finger of your other hand below the quilt. To end a line of quilting, take a tiny back stitch, make another small knot and pull between the layers. Make another inch-long stitch through the top and batting only and clip thread at the surface of the quilt. Carefully pull out the basting threads when the quilting is finished.

BINDING

Trim the edges of the quilt. Cut the binding fabric into seven 3in strips, selvedge to selvedge. Join

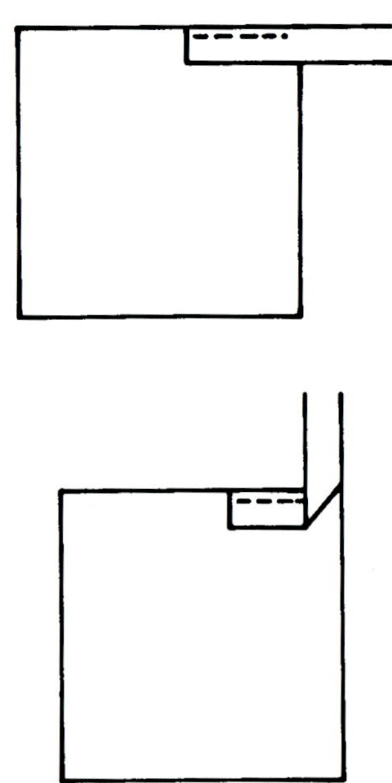

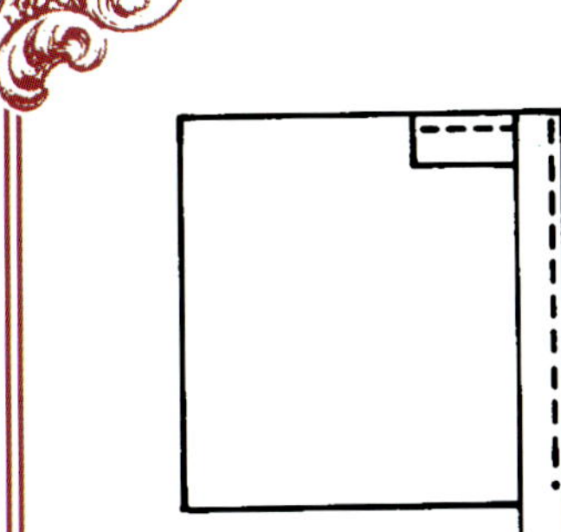

the strips to make one long strip and iron in half along the length, wrong sides together. Sew to the quilt top, starting at the centre bottom, ½in from the raw edges. To mitre the binding, stop ½in from the corner, back stitch and take out of machine. Fold the binding up making a 45 degree angle with the binding strip. Fold down, level with the edge and sew to the next corner. Repeat and overlap the ends of the binding. Slip stitch in place to the back of the quilt. A nice finishing touch is to embroider your name, city and date on the back of the quilt.

CARE OF QUILTS

Having spent so many hours of work on making a quilt you will obviously want to look after it in the best possible way. Remember, it may well become an heirloom in the future.

Whilst you obviously want to use and enjoy your quilt you also want to minimise the amount of wear and tear it receives. It is a good idea to get into the habit of folding back the quilt at night so it lies across the foot of the bed only. Or remove it entirely. In this age of electric blankets and heated waterbeds, a quilt is often decorative rather than functional. If you do need the quilt for warmth at night, use a sheet under it. Turn it back over the top edge of the quilt with at least a metre turn back; this will greatly reduce soiling. Quilts made from suitable fabrics can be successfully washed, but it is still worthwhile caring for the quilt to reduce frequent washing.

Sunlight weakens the fibres of fabric and also fades the colours. If the bed receives a lot of direct sunlight it may be wise to fold back the quilt or draw the curtains.

STORAGE

Store your quilt by rolling or folding it and wrapping in an old cotton pillowcase or sheet. If it is folded, it should be refolded occasionally along different fold lines to avoid making permanent creases. Never store in a plastic bag as air circulation is essential. Do not place an unwrapped quilt directly on a wooden shelf as chemicals in the timber can stain the fabric.

WASHING

If possible, hand wash the quilt in a large container such as the bath. Use warm, not hot, water and dissolve the detergent before adding the quilt. Soak for 5 to 10 minutes then squeeze gently by hand; do not twist or wring. Rinse thoroughly in lukewarm water. If you want to use fabric conditioner make sure it is stirred into the rinse water and not poured directly onto the quilt.

If you have a washing machine which is large enough to take the quilt without having to cram it in, it is a good idea to spin the quilt to remove excess water, as the excess weight of water can strain the stitching. Use a low speed spin if you have the option.

Dry the quilt outdoors away from direct sunlight, spread flat on a clean sheet, or drape it over a patio table. If using the clothesline, spread the quilt over several parallel lines rather than hanging the entire weight from one line.

The quilt can be machine washed if you do not have a large enough container. However, do not try to wash a large quilt in a small machine as it cannot be cleaned effectively and the lack of space can damage the quilt.

Once the quilt is dry, it can be placed in a tumble dryer on a no heat cycle to fluff up the batting.

If the quilt needs to be ironed, place it right side down on a thick towel and steam press gently on the wrong side. *

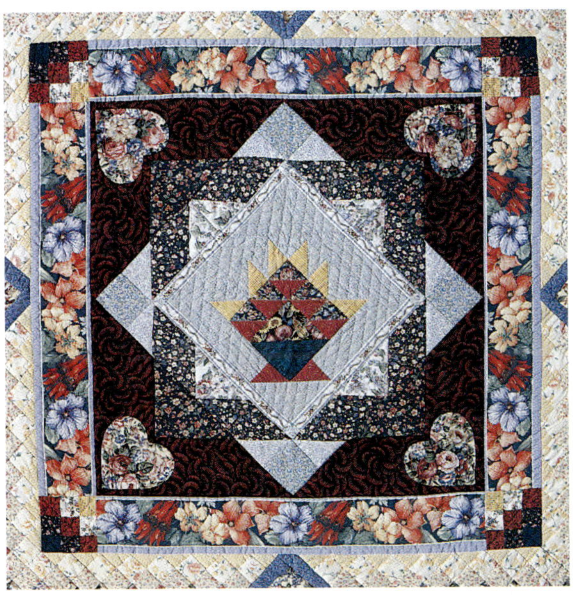

Acknowledgements

The Centenary Antique Centre, Centenary Road, Newcastle for generously allowing us to use their premises for photography. A great place for finding treasures to add to your collection. Definitely worth the trip!

Anita Crane from The Bear Lace Cottage, Park City, Utah USA for her two beautiful bears shown on the cover.

Yan Pring's daughter, Miranda, for her assistance in compiling all the drawings.

My very special thanks to Jan Vandenbergh for pulling it all together.

This wonderful book would not have been possible without the inspiration and motivation of Yan Pring. Yan has been a "Friend of the Store" for a long time and I'm sure sometimes wonders if the promotion to a "Friend of Gloria's" is better or worse! Yan teaches Quick Piecing Patchwork at Anne's Glory Box and has many devoted students. As well, I consider her to be the "Queen of Colourwash".

Gloria McKinnon

Editor
Gloria McKinnon

Assistant Editor
Kirsty Holmes

Photography
Mark Heriot, Chris Patterson

Styling
Fay King, Gloria McKinnon
Yan Pring

Design and Production
Joanne Martin

Illustrations
Lesley Griffith, Annette Tamone

Publisher
Sue Aiken

Published by
Express Publications Pty Ltd
A.C.N. 057 807 904

2 Stanley Street,
Silverwater
NSW 2128
Tel: (02) 9748 0599
Fax: (02) 9748 1956

Express Publications ISBN 1-875625-01-1